JAMS
PRESERVES AND
PICKLES

Rosemary Hume and
Muriel Downes

WEATHERVANE
BOOKS

Contents

★

CHAPTER I

Jams, Conserves and Marmalades

GOOD HOME-MADE jam is a luxury which everyone can enjoy, and indeed in these days when there is plenty of fresh fruit and sugar available, every housewife should have a variety of jams to show at the end of the season.

Jams may be divided into two categories, jam as we know it and conserves.

Conserves, or preserves as they are sometimes called, were much in vogue over a hundred years ago when fruit bottling was little known, and was a method of preserving whole or sliced fruit in syrup. Conserves were eaten, as they are abroad today, with a spoon, rather than spread on bread and butter.

The consistency of a good conserve is as a rule a little more syrupy than the ordinary jam and sweeter and richer in flavour.

As in most branches of cooking, certain rules must be observed when making jam in order to get a good result. They are simple and if read before starting on the recipes, your jam making should be more than successful.

RULES FOR JAM MAKING

1 Use dry, barely ripe fruit and either loaf (preserving sugar) or granulated sugar, as this helps the colour and the keeping power of the preserves.
2 Wash or wipe the fruit according to the kind, and pick it over.

3 Warm the sugar before adding to the boiling fruit, as this prevents lowering the temperature and consequent overcooking of the jam. Soft fruit gathered fresh from the garden needs less preliminary cooking than bought fruit.

4 When the sugar is completely dissolved, but not before, boil briskly, stirring gently and slowly until the jam sets on trial. Boiling too long darkens the colour and spoils the flavour of the jam. To test the jam remove the pan from the heat and put a little on a plate and cool it quickly. Run the little finger through the centre and if the jam is ready it will crinkle slightly and remain in two separate portions. It will also form a drop on the finger which will not fall.

5 Skim the jam if necessary towards the end of cooking only, as continuous skimming is unnecessary and wasteful.

6 Have the jam jars perfectly clean, dry and warm before filling, and fill quite full to allow for shrinkage. In the case of strawberries or cherries, to avoid the fruit rising, leave to stand 20-30 minutes to thicken, stir up and then pour into the jam jars.

7 Wipe the jars carefully with a cloth wrung out in very hot water. Tie down, label, and store in a cool dry place.

8 The setting power depends on the amount of pectin in the fruit being used. This is a natural gum-like substance and is found only in small quantities in strawberries, cherries, raspberries and vegetable marrow, but is plentiful in blackcurrants, redcurrants, gooseberries, damsons and apples.

9 The amount of pectin in any fruit is always greater when the fruit is slightly under-ripe.

10 When using fruit with a very low pectin content it is advisable to use one of the following ingredients to be

certain that your jam will set.

(a) The acid juice of gooseberries, apples or redcurrants.

(b) Commercially prepared pectin.

(c) Tartaric or citric acid added either in powder form dissolved in a little water, or the latter in the form of lemon juice.

Reasons for Jam not Keeping

Mildew may be caused by:

1 Using wet, cold jars.
2 Covering when neither hot nor cold.
3 Insufficient sealing when covering.
4 Storing in a damp place.

Crystallisation may be caused by:

1 Using too much sugar.
2 Allowing the jam to boil before all the sugar has dissolved.
3 Too much stirring when boiling.
4 Leaving uncovered too long.

Fermentation may be caused by:

1 Insufficient boiling.
2 Too little sugar used.
3 Storing in a warm place.

EQUIPMENT FOR JAM AND JELLY MAKING

The most important piece of equipment is the preserving pan. This may be of copper or aluminium. On the whole the latter is the most useful as both jams and chutnies can be made in it. Two preserving pans are ideal, one smaller than the other, for small batches of fruit or jelly.

Glass jam jars of good quality. Small honey jars 4-8 oz. These have metal covers and are particularly suitable for special jellies, mint, rowan, and so on.

A Jam Funnel or Filling Funnel. These are 4-5 in. across at the top with a 1½-2 in. tube and are extremely useful for filling the jam or jelly into the jars. They prevent any stickiness on the outside of the jars and avoid any possibility of scalding.

Several large wooden spoons, kept specially for jam or chutney. Wooden spoons can be bought with a notch in the handle to catch on the side of the preserving pan and so prevent the spoon from sliding into the jam.

Jam spoons have a wide bowl and may be bought in varying sizes.

Jam covers in cellophane, parchment, etc., and wax tissue for laying on the surface of the jam itself. Rubber bands or fine string for tying down.

Labels – the pots should be clearly labelled with the date of making. Proper covering and labelling adds a great deal to the attractiveness of the jam or jelly.

A flannel jelly bag or a piece of linen for straining fruit for jelly making.

A jelly stand is a help, particularly if a jelly bag is used.

A nylon sieve for fruit purées.

Butter muslin or cheese cloth.

Apple Ginger (1)

4 lb apples: 3 lb brown sugar: 1 oz whole ginger: pared rind and juice of two lemons.

Peel, quarter and core the apples. Bruise the ginger thoroughly by pounding or beating it in a mortar, or with a rolling pin.

Place the apples and sugar in layers in an earthenware crock or bowl, adding the ginger and lemon rind tied in a bundle, and the juice.

Cover and leave 48 hours.

Then turn into a preserving pan, bring to the boil and boil rapidly for 20–30 minutes or until a little will set when tested. Remove ginger and lemon rind, and pour into warm jars.

Tie down when cold.

This is a good preserve for a lunch sandwich with cheese.

Apple Ginger (2)

6 lb sour cooking apples: 2 oz root ginger: rind and juice of three lemons: ½ lb preserved ginger: 5 lb sugar.

Peel and core the apples, put the skins and cores in a pan with just enough water to cover and simmer until the skins are soft. Strain off the liquid, slice the apples thinly and put them in a preserving pan with the strained liquid and the grated rind and the juice of the lemons and the bruised root ginger tied in a muslin bag. Simmer gently until the apples are soft. Remove the root ginger and add the sugar and the preserved ginger, cut in small pieces. Stir until the sugar is dissolved, then bring the jam to the boil, stirring constantly and boil until a little sets on a plate.

Fresh Apricot Jam

6 lb apricots: ½ pint water: 6½ lb sugar.

Wash the fruit, cut in half and remove the stones. Tie half the stones in a small piece of muslin and remove the kernels from the remainder.

Place the fruit and water in a preserving pan and cook gently until the fruit is tender. Add the warmed sugar, heat until dissolved and then add the stones tied in muslin

11

and boil rapidly for about 25 minutes, or until the jam sets when tested. Skim if necessary, add the prepared kernels and pour into warm, dry jars. Tie down.

Dried Apricot Jam

1½ lb dried apricots: 2 quarts water: 4 lb sugar: 2 oz blanched almonds.

Wash the apricots, cover with the water and leave to soak for 48 hours. Turn into a preserving pan, bring slowly to the boil and then add the warm sugar. When the sugar has completely dissolved, boil briskly for 1 hour, adding the halved almonds 10 minutes before the end of the cooking time. Pour into warm, dry jars, and tie down when cold.

Blackcurrant Jam

4 lb blackcurrants: 2 lb water: 5 lb crushed preserving or granulated sugar.

Wash and stalk the currants, put them into the preserving pan with the water and simmer gently for a good hour or until thoroughly soft, then add the warmed sugar, stir occasionally until boiling and boil rapidly until the jam will set – about 15-20 minutes. Pour into warm, dry jars. Tie down.

Berry Jam

2 lb blackberries: 2 lb elderberries: 3 lb sugar.

Wash the blackberries and strip the elderberries from the stalks. Put into the preserving pan and crush with a wooden spoon to make the juice run. Bring slowly to the boil and cook 20 minutes. Add the warmed sugar, stir until dissolved and boil rapidly for 20 minutes. Pour into warm, dry jars.

Blackberry and Apple Jam

6 lb blackberries: 2 lb apples (weighed when peeled and cored): 8 lb sugar: ¼ pint lemon juice: 1 pint water.

Simmer blackberries and sliced apples, with peel and pips tied in muslin, with the water until soft and pulpy. Add lemon juice and sugar and boil rapidly until jam sets when tested.

Spiced Black Cherry Jam with Orange

4 good seedless oranges: 4 lb black cherries: 1 good gill of lemon juice: 2 sticks cinnamon: 6 cloves: 3½ lb granulated sugar.

Slice the oranges thinly. Put into a pan with water to cover by about ¼ in., and the spices tied in a muslin bag. Simmer until the oranges are really tender, then remove the bag. Meantime stone the cherries, crack a few of the stones and blanch the kernels. Add them to the pan with the cherries, lemon juice and sugar. Stir until the sugar is dissolved, then boil rapidly until thick. Turn into warm jars, and tie down when cold.

Morello Cherry Jam

4 lb Morello cherries: 1 teaspoon tartaric acid: 3 lb crushed preserving sugar: small tea cup of water.

Stone fruit and tie stones in a muslin bag. Put the fruit into a preserving pan with water and stones. Simmer gently until the cherries are tender, then add tartaric acid followed by the dissolved sugar. Boil rapidly until it will set when tested. Turn into warm, dry jars, and tie down.

Damson Jam

6 lb damsons: 7 lb sugar: 1 pint water.

Simmer the damsons in the water, very gently, about 20 minutes, until soft. Add sugar, and boil rapidly until it sets when tested. Most of the stones can be skimmed from the top of the jam during boiling. Turn into warm, dry jars. Tie down.

Gooseberry Jam

6 lb gooseberries: 8 lb sugar: 2 pints water.

Wash, top and tail gooseberries. Place in the preserving pan with the water and stew gently until soft and mushy – about 20 minutes. Add warmed sugar, dissolve slowly and then boil rapidly 15-20 minutes or until the jam sets when tested. Skim and pour into warm, dry jars.

Greengage Jam

6 lb greengages: ½ pint water: 6¼ lb sugar.

Wash the fruit, cut in half and remove the stones. Tie half the stones in a small piece of muslin and remove the kernels from the remainder.

Place the fruit and water in a preserving pan and cook gently until the fruit is tender. Add the warmed sugar, heat until dissolved and then add the stones tied in muslin and boil rapidly for about 25 minutes, or until the jam sets when tested. Skim if necessary, add the prepared kernels and pour into warm, dry jars. Tie down.

Loganberry Jam

4 lb loganberries: 4 lb sugar.

Hull the loganberries, wash quickly and carefully in a colander. Place in preserving pan and heat gently until the juice begins to flow. Add the warmed sugar, dissolve slowly and then boil rapidly until it sets when tested. Pour at once into warm, dry jars.

Seville Orange Marmalade

1 dozen Seville oranges: cold water: crushed preserving sugar.

Wipe oranges, quarter, remove pips, and cut into thin slices. Weigh this pulp, and measure 3 pints of water to every lb. Put all together, with the pips tied in muslin, into a large bowl and leave for 24 hours; then simmer until the peel is thoroughly soft. This will take 4-5 hours. Pour into bowl and leave 12 hours. Weigh pulp and allow 1-1¼ lb sugar to every lb. Bring slowly to the boil, stir to dissolve the sugar; boil rapidly until a little will set on testing. Pour off into pots and tie down.

N.B. If the marmalade is preferred with a lot of jelly use the larger proportion of sugar. The colour will be improved if the preserving pan is rubbed over with a cut lemon.

Marrow and Pineapple Jam

Peel the marrow, remove the seeds and cut into long narrow strips; weigh, and to every pound of marrow add ¾ lb granulated sugar. Leave in a stone jar or earthenware crock overnight. The next day, turn into a preserving pan and add 1 small tin pineapple chunks to every 3 lb marrow, cutting each 'chunk' in two or three pieces.

Bring slowly to the boil, stirring to make sure all the sugar has dissolved and then boil briskly for 2 hours. Test for setting, then pot and seal in the usual way.

Rhubarb and Pineapple Jam

10 lb rhubarb: 1 large tin pineapple: 10 lb loaf sugar.

Wipe and trim the rhubarb, cut into small pieces and place in a preserving pan with the juice from the pineapple; boil for $\frac{1}{2}$ hour. Add the sugar and the pineapple cut into pieces, dissolve over gentle heat and then boil briskly for about 20 minutes or until the jam sets when tested.

Marrow Jam

Make as for Marrow and Ginger, omitting the ginger.

Plum Jam

6 lb plums: $\frac{1}{2}$ pint water: $6\frac{1}{2}$ lb sugar.

Wash the fruit, cut in half, and remove the stones. Tie half the stones in a small piece of muslin and remove the kernels from the remainder. Place the fruit and water in a preserving pan and cook gently until the fruit is tender. Add the warmed sugar, heat until dissolved and then add the stones tied in muslin; boil rapidly for about 25 minutes or until the jam sets when tested. Skim if necessary, add the prepared kernels and pour into warm, dry jars.

Plum Jam (2)

This is a particularly juicy plum jam, soft and rich.

6 lb plums: $\frac{3}{4}$-1 lb preserving sugar to every lb of fruit.

Split plums with a stainless steel knife and remove the stones. Weigh the fruit and allow $\frac{3}{4}$-1 lb sugar to every pound of fruit. Put the fruit and half the sugar in layers in an earthenware bowl and leave overnight. Turn into a preserving pan and bring slowly to the boil. Simmer with the stones tied in a muslin bag until the plums are tender, add remaining sugar and boil rapidly until a little will set when tested – about 20-30 minutes. Remove the stones and pot.

N.B. This recipe can be used for damsons and bullaces, when the fruit is cooked whole and the stones removed.

Quince Jam

6 lb quinces: water: pared rind and juice of two lemons: sugar.

Peel, quarter and cut the quinces into small chunks. Put into the pan, cover with water, and simmer until quite soft (about 1 hour) with the pared rind of lemon in a muslin bag. Measure pulp, remove the lemon rind and allow 1 lb of sugar to 1 pint of pulp. Return to the pan with the lemon juice, allow to dissolve over low heat, then boil rapidly, stirring frequently until a little will set when tested. This should take about 15-20 minutes. Turn into warm jars and tie down.

Rhubarb and Ginger Jam

7 lb rhubarb (weighed after removing leaf and bottom of stalk): 3 large cooking apples: 5¼ lb sugar: 2 oz candied peel: 2 oz crystallised ginger: 1 lemon.

Wipe and cut up the rhubarb; peel, core and slice the apples; mix all with the sugar and leave on a large dish overnight. Turn into a preserving pan, add the finely chopped peel and shredded ginger, the grated rind and juice of the lemon and bring slowly to the boil. Boil quickly until a little will set when tried on a cold plate.

Marrow and Ginger Jam

1 oz root ginger: 8 lb marrow (weighed after peeling and seeding): 6 lb preserving or granulated sugar: pared rind and juice of 4 lemons.

Cut the marrow into inch cubes. Place in a bowl with layers of sugar and leave for 24 hours. Put into preserving pan, with the lemon rind and well bruised ginger tied in a muslin bag. Bring slowly to the boil and remove the muslin bag when the ginger and lemon flavour is strong enough. Boil gently until the syrup is thick and the marrow clear and transparent, stirring frequently to ensure that the jam does not stick to the bottom of the pan. Pour into warm, dry jars. Seal.

Rhubarb and Orange Jam

6 lb rhubarb, trimmed and cut up into small pieces: 2 oranges: 4½ lb. granulated sugar.

Spread the rhubarb in a bowl in layers with the sugar and leave for twelve hours. Boil the oranges whole until they are just tender. Cut into quarters, removing the pips, then slice finely. Place in a preserving pan with the rhubarb and sugar and stir over gentle heat. When the sugar has dissolved, boil rapidly until the jam will set when tested.

Tomato Jam

6 lb tomatoes: 6 lb sugar: 10 tablespoonsful.lemon juice: the pith and rind of two lemons, or 2 level teaspoons of powdered tartaric or citric acid.

18

Scald tomatoes to remove the skin. Slice or quarter and put them into a pan (do not use copper), add the lemon juice and pith and rind or acid. Simmer until pulpy. Warm sugar, add to pan, stir until dissolved, then boil rapidly until the jam will set on testing. Turn into warm jars and tie down. This jam may be made with red or green tomatoes.

Raspberry Jam

6 lb raspberries: 6 lb crushed preserving or granulated sugar.

Put the fruit into the pan, set on a slow fire to draw out the juice. Have the sugar warmed and add carefully to the fruit; bring slowly to the boil and stir occasionally. When the sugar is completely dissolved, bring rapidly to boiling point and when this is reached, draw aside, pot and tie down when cold.

N.B. This is particularly good, fresh-tasting jam, and as a rule keeps very well. However, if the season has been wet and the fruit itself full of moisture, mould may be inclined to form on the top of the jam. If this is so, the jam must be watched carefully and any mould removed at once. The jam must actually boil and so it is advisable to use a thermometer to make sure that it does so. If a thermometer is not available, stir the jam two or three times round, just before the boil.

Raspberry Jam (2)

6 lb dry sound raspberries: 7½ lb preserving or granulated sugar.

Put the fruit into the preserving pan, set on gentle heat and bring slowly to the boil. Boil for not longer than 2-3 minutes, then add the sugar, previously warmed. Stir until melted, then pour rapidly into jars, wipe round and cover when cold.

Raspberry Jam (3)

A recipe taken from a manuscript book dated 1827.

To every pound of raspberries take 1½ lb of lump sugar beaten fine. Mash the raspberries well, put with the sugar in layers in an earthenware bowl, and leave two nights and a day, stirring from time to time. The sugar must be quite dissolved. Put into a preserving pan and stir constantly to boiling point, but on no account let it actually boil. Put into pots at once. Tie down when cold.

Strawberry Jam

4 lb strawberries: 4 lb granulated sugar or finely crushed preserving sugar: juice of 1 lemon: ½ oz fresh butter.

Crush a small saucerful of the berries with a silver fork and put into the bottom of a preserving pan with a large spoonful of the sugar. Melt on a slow fire, then add the remaining fruit and bring to the boil, stirring occasionally. Add the previously warmed sugar to the pan with the strained juice of the lemon. Boil rapidly for about 12-15 minutes. Test for setting and stir in the butter to finish. Pour into warm, dry jars and tie down.

Strawberry Jam (2)

4 lb strawberries: 4 lb sugar: ½ pint redcurrant or gooseberry juice (for method of preparing juice see *Rules for Jelly Making*).

Hull the strawberries and wash carefully in a colander.

Drain well and place in a preserving pan with the sugar and heat gently until dissolved. Add the fruit juice and boil rapidly till setting point is reached. Remove from the heat, leave to stand 20-30 minutes to thicken, stir up and pour into warm, dry jars and tie down when quite cold.

Whole Fruit Marmalade

Boil Seville oranges whole until very tender. This will take about 1 hour and a good test is when the head of a pin will go easily into the skin. Cut fruit into quarters and remove the pips, then slice. To every lb of fruit add 1 pint of water, then weigh again and add to each lb 1 lb of sugar. Dissolve over slow heat, then boil rapidly until marmalade will set when tested. Pour into warm, dry jars and tie down.

Grapefruit Marmalade

3 grapefruits: 3 oranges: 3 lemons: water and sugar: good pinch of salt.

Choose thin-skinned fruit and wash thoroughly. Quarter the fruit and slice very thinly, saving the pips. Measure the fruit and juice and add three times the quantity of water and the pips tied in a muslin bag. Cover and simmer for two hours, then stand overnight. Measure and add an equal amount of sugar, add the salt, put all together into the pan and heat over a slow fire; stir occasionally and, when the sugar has dissolved, boil rapidly until a little of the marmalade will set when tested. Remove from the fire and allow to stand 1 hour, stirring several times to distribute the peel evenly. Put into pots and tie down.

Orange Marmalade

8 Seville oranges: 3 sweet oranges: 2 lemons: 9 pints water: 8 lb sugar.

Cut the oranges and lemons in two, squeeze the juice and place the pips in a small muslin bag. Cut the skin and pulp into fine shreds or put through the mincer; place in a large earthenware bowl with the water and pips and leave to soak for 24 hours. Place all in a preserving pan and boil for two hours or until the pulp has reduced by half. Squeeze the liquid from the small muslin bag; add the warm sugar, dissolve slowly and then boil rapidly for about half an hour or until the marmalade sets when tested. Pour into warm, dry jars. Tie down.

Ginger Marmalade

(Made with an apple jelly base).

4 lb cooking apples or windfalls: 2 pints water: 1 lb sugar to 1 pint juice: 1 oz root ginger, bruised and tied in a muslin bag: preserved ginger, about 4 oz to each pint of juice.

Wash and cut up the apples, stew to a pulp with the water and root ginger. Turn all into a cloth or jelly bag and allow the juice to drip through. Measure juice and add the sugar. Dissolve over slow heat then boil rapidly for about 7 minutes. Test for setting and when it 'jells', add the preserved ginger cut into dice. Reboil and pot.

NOTE: The amount of ginger mentioned is only approximate – it should be added according to taste and, the strength of the ginger.

Quince Marmalade

7 lb quinces: water: 7 lbs sugar.

Weigh the fruit, then peel, core and quarter it, reserving the peelings. Put fruit into a pan with about a pint of water, cover tightly and cook gently in the oven until it is pink in colour and quite soft. In the meantime, put peelings into a pan with a pint of water, cover and cook until soft, then strain. Put this juice into the preserving pan, add the weight of the fruit in sugar, and heat, stirring until dissolved. Then add the quince pulp and boil gently, stirring constantly, for about half an hour or until the marmalade will set. Pour into small jars or moulds and tie down.

This may be turned out and eaten with cream cheese.

Pear Marmalade

6 lb pears: 4½ lb loaf sugar.

Peel, halve and remove the cores from the pears. Set the peelings and cores on one side, place the pears in a stewpan with sufficient water to cover and cook until tender. Lift out the pears with a draining spoon, put the peelings and cores into the pan, boil hard until reduced by half and then strain. Dissolve the sugar in the liquid and boil till it 'jellies on the spoon'; replace the pears and boil up. Stir for a few minutes until the marmalade is smooth, then pour into warm, dry jars. Tie down when quite cold.

CONSERVES

Black Cherry Conserve

4 lb cherries: 2¼ lb sugar: 1 rounded teaspoon citric acid or scant ¼ pint lemon juice.

Stone the cherries, crack about 2 dozen of the stones, add the kernels, blanched and skinned, to the fruit with the sugar, and stand overnight. Barely cover the rest of the stones with water, boil 30-40 minutes and strain. Keep the water, add to the cherries with the acid or lemon juice and bring slowly to the boil. Then boil hard for about half an hour until set. Turn into warm pots, cover with a waxed paper dipped in brandy and then with parchment or cellophane covers.

Strawberry Conserve

The strawberries for this ought to be picked right from the garden. They must be perfect. A thermometer is necessary for complete success.

5 lb strawberries, weighed after picking over and hulling: 5 lb granulated sugar: 1¾ pints of water.

Dissolve the sugar in the water slowly, in a copper preserving pan. When it has completely dissolved boil rapidly to the soft ball degree (234-238° F.). Add the fruit, place a cover over the pan, remove from the heat and allow the strawberries to soak in the syrup for quarter of an hour. Return to the heat, bring rapidly to the boil until the syrup boils up over the fruit. Draw off the heat and allow the syrup to subside. Skim if necessary. Repeat this process of bringing to the boil, drawing off the heat and skimming twice more. Remove the strawberries with a pierced spoon, and spread them in a single layer on a wire sieve, putting a large plate or a dish under the sieve to catch the syrup. The syrup is scraped back into the pan and reduced by rapid boiling until a drop will set on a plate. Return the strawberries and boil for 5 minutes. Put into hot, dry jars.

A few cloves tied in a muslin bag are often cooked with this jam.

Strawberry Conserve (2)

3 lb strawberries: 3 lb sugar: ¾ pint red currant juice.

Hull the strawberries, cover with sugar and leave overnight in a warm place in order to draw out the juice. (This may also be done in a cool oven for a few hours.) Place fruit and red currant juice in preserving pan, bring to the boil and boil rapidly until setting point is reached.

Peach Slices in Jelly

Thin slices of ripe peaches: apple jelly flavoured with lemon, lemon verbena or rose geranium.

Make a good apple jelly, flavoured with lemon or leaves of rose geranium or lemon verbena (for method see Quince Jelly, page 31). Peel the peaches, slice thinly and drop into the jelly when it has almost reached setting point (after about 15-20 minutes boiling). Simmer gently for a few minutes, then boil rapidly until the slices are cooked and the jelly sets.

The proportion of jelly to peaches is a matter of taste; but the appearance and flavour are better if the jelly is not too full of peaches.

Pippins in Orange Jelly

About 12 pippins (Allington, Ribston or Cox, small and even-sized: 6-7 lb cooking apples for the jelly): thinly pared rind of 1 orange: loaf sugar: flavouring, such as scented mint leaves, rose geranium, or lemon verbena.

Choose small, even-sized pippins, wash, pare and core them carefully. Boil the cores and peel in sufficient water to just float the pippins and poach them until tender. Remove, cover and set aside. Wash and cut the cooking apples into small pieces without removing the peel or core. Place in a pan with the juice from the pippins and sufficient water to come within 1 inch of the top of the apples. Simmer to a pulp, strain through a nylon sieve or cloth. Measure the juice and allow 1 lb sugar to 1 pint juice. Place both in a shallow pan, bring to the boil, skim well, boil 2-3 minutes.

Carefully add the pippins with flavouring tied in a muslin bag. Simmer very gently until the pippins become semi-transparent. Meantime, simmer orange peel in water until tender. Drain well. Remove the pippins, wrap a piece of peel round each and pack carefully into wide-necked jars.

Boil jelly rapidly until it will just set (after removing the muslin). Pour over apples to cover, leave till cold and tie down tightly.

Preserved Peaches

10-12 Yellow Clingstone peaches: 3 lb sugar: 1 qt water.

First prepare a sugar syrup with 1 qt water and $1\frac{1}{4}$ lb of the sugar. Skin the peaches and cut into even slices. Place the fruit in the syrup and cook gently until the fruit is tender but in no way soft. Remove from the heat and cool quickly by standing the pan in a bowl of cold water. Set aside for 24 hours, then add a further 11 oz of the sugar, dissolve over gentle heat and boil carefully for two minutes. Remove from the heat, cool quickly and stand aside for 24 hours. Add remaining sugar, dissolve slowly, and again boil for two minutes. Remove from the heat, allow to cool to form a skin and then stir two or three times to even out the fruit. Pour into hot jars and seal at once.

N.B. This recipe is also suitable for apricots, fresh pineapple, strawberries and greengages.

Black Cherry Conserve

4 lb black cherries: 2 oranges: 6 tablespoons lemon juice: 2 lb sugar: 6 cloves (optional): ¾ teaspoonful ground cinnamon.

Slice oranges very thinly, removing the pips. Barely cover slices with water and cook until quite tender. Stone the cherries and add with all the other ingredients and cook until thick and clear. Pour into warm, dry pots and seal.

Quince Conserve

6 lb quinces: cane sugar.

Peel and quarter the fruit. Remove the core. Cut across into slices about one-eighth inch thick. If the quinces are large, first cut the quarter of fruit in half lengthways.

Reserve the peelings and cores, wash, put into a pan, cover with water and simmer 25-30 minutes, then strain. Put the sliced quince into this water and simmer until three parts cooked. Make sure the liquor covers the slices. It is best to cook the quince in 2 or 3 lots to avoid breaking the slices. The raw quince may be put in water with 2 oz salt to the gallon to prevent them from getting brown while they are waiting to be cooked. Rinse well before adding to the pan. Strain the cooked quince carefully, keeping the slices separate.

Now measure the quince liquor, and to this add 2 lb sugar to 1 pint of liquor. Dissolve the sugar carefully, then bring to the boil. Skim and add the sliced quince. Simmer gently until the slices become clear and the syrup is very thick when tested. Pour off into a bowl and pot when almost cold. Tie down when quite cold.

★

CHAPTER II

Jellies, Fruit Cheeses and Butters

JELLIES

FOR JELLY-MAKING the juice of the fruit only is used and the fruits most suitable are those with good setting power and with a strong natural flavour, such as red and black currants, raspberries, plums, damsons and crab apples. Cooking apples and windfalls particularly, are excellent for jelly-making and here a second ingredient in the form of fruit or herb, to give extra flavour and colour, is a good addition.

Choice and Preparation of Fruit

1 Fruit for jelly-making should never be over-ripe; in fact it is better to err on the side of under-ripeness to get a really good 'set'.
2 Soft fruit, such as currants, need only be washed in a colander. After draining, they are ready for the stone jar or double saucepan and it is not necessary to remove the stalks.
3 Hard fruit should be washed and wiped and, if very large, cut into rough pieces. Do not remove the peel or core from apples as these are a valuable source of pectin and improve the 'set' of the jelly.

The juice of the fruit for jelly-making is extracted in the following way.

Soft Fruits

Here the juice is obtained without the addition of water.

1 Place the fruit in a stone jar, crush lightly with a wooden spoon, cover with a plate and EITHER stand in a deep pan of water and simmer gently for about one hour, until all the juice is extracted, OR, cook in a very slow oven.

For a small quantity of fruit this can be done quite satisfactorily in a double saucepan.

Hard Fruits

1 Place the fruit in a preserving pan, add water to reach about a quarter of the way up the fruit, crush with a wooden spoon and simmer gently until pulpy.
2 Turn the cooked fruit into a jelly bag or double linen cloth and leave to drain overnight. Do not disturb or press the fruit in the bag in any way.
3 The following day, measure the juice and allow one pound of preserving or loaf sugar to every one pint of juice, except for red and black currants, when as much as 1¼ lb can be used.
4 Heat the extracted juice, add the sugar gradually and stir until dissolved.
5 Boil rapidly and test for set after three minutes for soft fruit, and after 5 minutes for hard fruit, although the latter may need up to 10 minutes cooking, particularly if it is a wet season.
6 Skim immediately and pour at once into small warm pots. Work quickly at this stage as the jelly tends to set round the sides of the preserving pan.

Apple Jelly

6 lb tart cooking apples or crab-apples: 3 pints water:

1 lb sugar to every pint of juice: lemon rind to flavour.

Wash apples, wipe and cut into pieces, removing the bruised parts. Crab-apples may be left whole. Put into pan with the water, simmer until very soft, stirring and crushing the fruit occasionally. Turn on to a cloth to drip. Measure the extracted juice and add sugar in proportion. Stir over the heat until the sugar has dissolved. Add 2-3 strips of lemon rind, then boil rapidly until it will set when tested. Pour into small glass jars, removing the lemon rind. Tie down.

Apple jelly may be flavoured in various ways; rose geranium, lemon verbena, and mint for serving with roast lamb. For mint jelly, use the tart cooking apples rather than the crab-apples.

Rose Geranium Jelly

Make the above apple jelly with either crabs or ordinary apples. When the sugar has dissolved in the juice, add 3-4 rose geranium leaves tied together, continue to boil and remove the leaves when jelly is well flavoured.

Flavour in the same way with lemon verbena. Tie half a dozen or more leaves in a small muslin bag.

Mint Jelly

Make half the quantity of apple jelly recipe. When sugar has dissolved add a bunch of mint and boil until well flavoured. Just before potting, colour with a little green colouring. Pot in small jars.

Quince Jelly

6 lb quinces: water: pared rind and juice of 2 lemons: sugar.

Wash quinces and remove all blemished parts. Cut up and put into a pan with cold water to come barely level with the fruit. Simmer until pulpy. Turn into a jelly cloth or bag and leave overnight. Measure the juice and allow 1 lb sugar per pint of juice. Put together into a preserving pan, add strips of lemon rind tied together and the strained juice. Bring to the boil slowly, stirring from time to time to dissolve the sugar. Boil rapidly, skimming occasionally, until it will set when tested. Fill into warm jars and tie down. A piece of the peel may be put into each jar if wished.

Grape Jelly

4 lb grapes: 2 tablespoons lemon juice: 1 lb loaf sugar to each pint of juice: clove or cinnamon to flavour.

Crush grapes lightly and put them into a jar or pan and heat gently to extract the juice. Turn into a jelly bag or cloth and leave to drip overnight. Measure the juice, add sugar in proportion; add lemon juice and flavour, if liked, with a few cloves or sticks of cinnamon, tied in a muslin bag. Put this with the grape juice and sugar and stir until the sugar has dissolved, then boil until a little will set on a plate. Pour into small, warm glass jars and tie down.

Rowan Jelly

Rowan berries: apples: water: sugar: peeled rind of 1 lemon and 2 cloves, to not more than 2 quarts of juice, tied in a muslin bag.

The proportion of rowan berries to apples is about 2 lb to 1 lb of apples or to taste.

Pick berries from the stalks and wash. Wash, wipe and

slice the apples and put both into a pan with water to come level with the fruit.

Simmer until pulpy. Strain through a cloth or jelly bag. Measure the juice and allow 1 lb sugar to every pint. Put together into a copper preserving pan rubbed round with a piece of lemon. Bring to the boil, stirring occasionally, then add the flavouring and boil rapidly until a small quantity will crinkle when it is cold and pushed with the finger. Remove flavouring. Turn into small pots and tie down.

This jelly does not always have a firm and jelly-like set, depending on the proportion of apple and berries used. Serve with game or rich meats.

Damson Jelly

6 lb damsons: 3 pints of water: 1 lb sugar to 1 pint of juice.

Simmer fruit in water until pulpy. Drain to extract all the juice. Measure and add sugar in proportion. Dissolve sugar and boil rapidly until it sets when tested. Pot.

Elderberry and Apple Jelly

3 lb tart cooking apples (windfalls are particularly good): 2 qt elderberries, picked from their stalks: peeled rind of 1 orange and a half-stick of cinnamon, tied together with cotton: 2 pints water: sugar.

Wash the apples well and remove the blemished parts. Cut into pieces and put into a pan with the elderberries. Add water, cover the pan and simmer to a pulp. Turn into a cloth or jelly bag and leave to drip. Measure juice and allow 1 lb sugar to 1 pint juice. Put together into a pan, stir over moderate heat until dissolved, then add the orange rind and cinnamon. Boil rapidly until a little will crinkle on a saucer when it is cold and pushed with the finger. Remove flavouring, turn into warm jars and tie down.

This jelly should be of a soft, rather than too firm a consistency. The above recipe could be used for blackberry and apple jelly.

Gooseberry and Elderflower Jelly

This jelly has a pronounced muscat flavour.

6 lb green gooseberries: 1½ pints water: 1 lb sugar to 1 pint juice: 3-4 large elderflowers.

Wash gooseberries, put in pan with the water. Simmer till pulpy. Drain on cloth to extract all juice; measure; add the sugar and stir till dissolved. Boil and add 3-4 large elderflowers tied in a piece of muslin. Continue boiling until a little will set when tested. Remove flowers, pot and tie down.

Blackcurrant Jelly

6 lb blackcurrants: 2¼ pints water: 1 lb sugar to 1 pint juice.

Wash fruit, add water, and simmer until very soft. Drain in a cloth to extract all juice. Measure, and add the sugar in proportion, boil rapidly until set when tested. Pot and tie down.

Medlar Jelly

Ripe medlars: water: loaf or preserving sugar: lemons.

Peel and slice the medlars, put into a pan with water barely to cover. Simmer until the fruit is very tender. Turn all into a jelly bag or cloth. Leave for some hours. Measure juice and allow 1 lb of sugar and the juice of

1 lemon to each pint. Return to the pan with a few strips of the pared lemon rind tied together with a piece of cotton. Heat slowly until the sugar has dissolved, then boil rapidly until the jelly will set when tested. Remove lemon rind and pot.

Red Currant Jelly

6 lb red currants: castor or granulated sugar.

Pick off the currants into earthenware or kilner jars. Cover and put into a slow oven until the juice has run well. Turn into a jelly or muslin bag. Next day, measure the juice and weigh out 1 lb sugar to every pint of juice. Spread out the sugar on to trays, and put it into the oven to make it as hot as possible *without* colouring. Have ready the currant juice heated to boiling point (but on no account allow to boil), draw aside and add the sugar gradually, stirring all the time. When the sugar is melted, pour at once into pots.

Jelly made in this way keeps the flavour of the fresh fruit.

Orange Jelly

6 Seville oranges: 6 sweet oranges: 2 lemons: 12 pints water : loaf or preserving sugar.

Wipe and slice the fruit thinly, removing and reserving the pips. Tie these in a piece of muslin. Put all into a preserving pan with the water. Simmer until the liquid has reduced by half, three to four hours. Then turn into a jelly bag or linen cloth and leave until next day to drain. Measure juice, and allow 1 pint to 1 lb of sugar. Warm sugar, add to juice, dissolve over slow heat, then boil rapidly until it will set when tested.

Unripe Grape Jelly

Grape thinnings: loaf sugar.

Wash the grapes well, put the whole bunches in a stew-pan and cover with water. Stew gently for 1 hour. Drain through a jelly bag, and measure. Put the measured juice into the preserving pan and add 1 lb loaf sugar for every quart of juice. Bring quickly to the boil and simmer until the jelly is firm when a few drops are tested on a cold saucer. Pour into small pots and tie down when cold.

This jelly may be flavoured with a small piece of stick cinnamon if liked.

FRUIT CHEESES AND BUTTERS

Fruit cheeses and butters should be made with such fruit as damsons, apples, red plums, quinces, gooseberries, etc. Sometimes fruit cheeses are made from the pulp in the jelly bag after the juice has been extracted for jelly-making. This should only be done as an economy measure and is not really to be recommended. As most of the pectin has been drained away, the resulting 'cheese' has a poor set and is best used within a month of being made.

A fruit cheese is of a firmer and more solid consistency than a fruit butter. A cheese can be cut into slices or shapes, while a butter, as the name indicates, is of a soft, spreadable consistency. Although a cheese contains equal quantity of sugar to pulp, a butter has half that amount and is therefore made for immediate use.

These rules will indicate the process to be followed for making fruit cheeses and butters. Those not familiar with them will find that they are especially good with biscuit and butter, or with cream cheese as a finish to a lunch or supper.

1 Prepare the required quantity of fruit and place in the

preserving pan with water to come barely level with the fruit.

2 Simmer well until reduced and well pulped.

3 Rub the pulp through a sieve, preferably a hair or nylon sieve.

4 Measure the pulp and allow 1 lb sugar to each pint of pulp obtained.

5 Dissolve the sugar, boil, stirring constantly until setting stage is reached, then pot and tie down as for jam, in small jars or bowls.

Damson Cheese

(Make apple, apricot and quince cheese in the same way.)
Damsons: sugar: water.

Put the clean fruit in the pan, add water to come barely level with the fruit. Simmer gently until fruit is thoroughly soft and pulpy. Remove as many stones as possible. Rub the pulp through a nylon sieve. Weigh the pulp and allow 1 lb sugar to 1 lb pulp. Now boil gently about 1-1¼ hours until very thick, stirring constantly and taking care to scrape the bottom of the pan from time to time. Test for setting. Pot in small jars or bowls and tie down.

For use, turn out and cut into slices.

Cherry Butter

This is not sieved.

4 lb cherries: grated rind and juice of 1 lemon: 2 lb sugar.

Stone cherries, crack a reasonable number of the stones, extract the kernels, blanch and skin. Add the lemon to the fruit and put into a bowl with the sugar, in layers. Leave overnight. Bring to the boil, simmer 15-20 minutes, then boil rapidly until very thick. Turn into small pots, cover and tie down.

Apple and Plum Butter

3 lb apples: 1 lb plums: ¾ lb sugar to each pint of pulp.

Peel, core and cut apples, then cook in a little water until soft. Stone plums, add and cook until soft. Put through a sieve, add sugar and boil until setting. Pot at once.

Apricot Curd

½ lb apricots, fresh: 1 lemon: 2 oz butter: ½ lb castor sugar: very little water: 2 eggs.

Wash the fruit and put in a preserving pan with a very little water and cook until soft. Sieve. Put the fruit in a double saucepan, with the sugar, butter, the juice and grated rind of the lemon. When the sugar has dissolved, add the beaten eggs and stir the mixture until it thickens. Pour into hot jars and cover.

Lemon Curd

2 large lemons: 3 oz butter: ½ lb loaf sugar: 3 eggs.

Grate the lemon rind and strain the juice. Put into a double saucepan, add the butter, heat gently, then add the sugar. Beat the eggs and strain into the pan. Stir over heat until thick, then pour into clean dry jars. Tie down closely.

Apricot and Orange Cheese

1 lb best dried apricots: 1 large orange: 1 lb granulated sugar: granulated sugar for finishing.

Soak apricots overnight in water just to cover. Simmer until very soft. Boil orange until tender. Pass apricots through sieve and the orange through a mincer. Mix. Weigh the pulp, and allow same quantity of sugar. Put together into a pan or double boiler and cook until the mixture will set when tested. Turn into shallow trays lined with paper. When set, cut into rounds (peppermint cream size) and roll in granulated sugar. This may equally well be put into small bowls or pots for turning out.

Quince Marmalade or Paste

Ripe quinces. Peel and cut into small pieces. Cook until very soft in water barely to cover. Pass through a sieve. Weigh the purée and take the same weight in sugar. Mix sugar and purée and cook over low heat until thick. Pour into soup plates and leave to dry on the top of the stove or in an airing cupboard for 2 days. After this, turn the mixture upside down out of the plate and dry it again another two days. Sift castor sugar thickly over it and cut into little squares and put into a box with a layer of greaseproof paper between each layer.

Apple paste may be done exactly the same way with the addition of spice if liked.

A *marmalade* is a term for a much reduced fruit purée, cooked down with sugar – in fact a 'cheese'.

★

CHAPTER III

Spiced Fruits and Pickles

INTRODUCTION TO PICKLES – SWEET AND SOUR

PICKLES CAN be made in great variety and are a welcome addition to the table.

The rules and ingredients for success are simple – well-chosen fresh vegetables without blemish, good quality vinegar and careful and neat arrangement in the jars.

When they have been washed and prepared the vegetables are salted (i.e. sprinkled with dry salt, or soaked in brine). For this, use a good quality block salt – in preference to the packet salt – and grind down to a powder for use. An easy method is to cut the block in half and rub the halves together, or rub the block on a coarse grater.

After the preliminary salting, which is usually 12-24 hours, the vegetables may be rinsed in cold water or left salted. This is usually stated in the recipe.

Brine is a mixture of salt and water, and the strength varies according to the purpose for which it is to be used. Standard strength is 1 lb salt to 1 gallon boiling water. This is poured on to the salt, strained through a muslin and used when cold.

It is important to use a first quality vinegar for the making of pickles. This means that the vinegar will contain the correct amount of acetic acid to ensure that the vegetables will keep properly. Brown malt vinegar is the vinegar usually preferred as the pickles have a better flavour when preserved in it. White malt gives a better appearance as the colour and variety of the vegetables are more easily seen when in the jar.

White wine or cider vinegar may also be used, but are rather expensive to use for ordinary pickles.

Vinegar is usually spiced before pouring over the vegetables etc. to be pickled. This may, of course, be spiced when the pickle is being made, but it is more convenient to spice a certain amount of the vinegar well beforehand and keep it in bottles ready for use. Different combinations of spices for vegetables may be used, or pickling spice, a mixture of ready prepared spices, may be bought from the grocer.

A recipe for spiced vinegar is given here.

Vinegar may be poured over the vegetables, packed in the jars, either hot or cold. A general rule is to pour cold vinegar over vegetables that must be crisp when eaten, such as cabbage, and hot vinegar over the softer vegetables, such as cucumber.

Special jars can be bought for pickles, four square with lined screw lids, and these are well worth buying if pickles are to be made. They prevent the spilling and evaporation of the vinegar and are easy to pack and store.

Sauce ketchup bottles may also be bought; they are a convenience as they have screw tops and so are simple to sterilise.

Vinegars, pickles and chutnies should be made only in aluminium, stainless steel, or enamel pans, and should not come in contact with copper, brass or iron.

A wooden spoon should also always be used.

Spiced Vinegar

To keep for pickles.

These spices may be varied to taste, but the following

is an average mixture. If a hotter one is required, bruised root ginger and chillis may be added and an additional quantity of mustard seed.

To 1 quart vinegar take:

1 stick cinnamon: $\frac{1}{4}$ oz blade mace: $\frac{1}{2}$ oz black pepper-corns: $\frac{1}{4}$ oz allspice (Pimento or Jamaican pepper): $\frac{1}{2}$ oz mustard seed.

Tie the spices together in a small muslin bag. Put into an enamel pan with the vinegar. Cover the pan and bring slowly to the boil, but do not allow actually to bubble.

Draw off the heat and leave for 2 hours, to allow the flavour of the spices to get into the vinegar. Then remove bag and pour off the vinegar into bottles.

If using the bought pickling spice, allow between 2 and 3 oz to 1 quart of vinegar.

Garden Pickle

2 lb tomatoes: 1 lb onions: 1 small white cabbage: 1 small marrow: $\frac{1}{2}$ lb sugar: 2 oz dry mustard: $2\frac{1}{2}$ tablespoons curry powder: 2 lb small outdoor cucumbers: 2 cauli-flowers: 1 lb runner beans: $\frac{1}{4}$ lb flour: $4\frac{1}{2}$ tablespoons salt: 2 quarts vinegar.

Slice the tomatoes. Sprinkle them with salt and leave for 12 hours. Drain and wash. Wash and prepare the other vegetables, chop and shred them, put in a large pan, cover with boiling water and add 3 tablespoons salt. Simmer until all the vegetables are tender. Drain and cover with this mixture:

Mix flour, sugar, mustard, $1\frac{1}{2}$ tablespoons salt and curry powder. Blend to a thin cream with a little cold vinegar. Bring the rest of the vinegar to the boil and pour it on to this mixture. Stir well, return to the pan and cook for

43

5 minutes after it comes to the boil. Pour over the strained vegetables and simmer for 5 minutes. The mixture should cover the vegetables well. Pot and tie down while hot. Keep at least 6 months before using.

Marrow Pickle

4 lb marrow: 1 lb onions or shallots: 1 lb sugar: 2 pints vinegar: pickling spice: about 1 oz turmeric and about 3 oz flour mixed together with a little water.

Cut up onions and marrow, lay on a big dish, sprinkle well with salt and stand overnight. Pour off juice, wash if too salt. Cook with sugar, vinegar and pickling spice for 20-30 minutes, then thicken with turmeric and flour. Reboil.

Piccalilli

2 cauliflowers: 2 medium sized cucumbers: 16 French beans: 1 lb onions: 1 medium sized marrow: 1 quart vinegar: 1 oz whole spice: 4 oz Demerara sugar: ½ oz ground ginger: 1 oz mustard: ½ oz turmeric: 1 tablespoon flour.

Cut the vegetables into small pieces. Lay on a dish and sprinkle with salt. Leave 12 hours. Drain off the water, boil nearly all the vinegar with the spice, then strain. Mix the other ingredients, with the remaining cold vinegar, into a smooth paste: then mix with boiled vinegar. Pour into a saucepan, add vegetables, and boil for 15 minutes.

Chow-Chow

1 quart green small tomatoes: 2 green peppers: 1 bunch celery: 1 lb runner beans: 1 oz turmeric: ¼ oz pepper: salt: 6 small cucumbers: 1 small cauliflower: ½ lb small onions:

2 oz mustard seed: $\frac{1}{4}$ oz. allspice: $\frac{1}{4}$ oz. ground cloves:
2 quarts vinegar.

Prepare vegetables by cutting them in small pieces.
Cover with salt and leave for 24 hours. Put the spices in
the vinegar and bring to boiling point, add the vegetables
and simmer until tender.

Mixed Vegetable Pickle

Choose a mixture of button onions, sprigged cauliflower
and cubes of cucumber or any other mixture you prefer.
Allow 1-2 chillis per $\frac{1}{2}$ pint jar.

Lay all the vegetables on a dish, sprinkle very well with
dry salt, almost to cover them, and leave 48 hours before
draining off all the liquid. Pack into jars in an attractive
pattern and fill up with a cold spiced vinegar. This is
ready to use after 14 days.

Pickled Nasturtium Seeds

Choose the large green fruits, soak them in brine for 24
hours. Drain and pack straight away in small jars. Pour
in boiling spiced vinegar and seal down at once. It is
advisable to put them into screw-top jars as they should
be air-tight.

Serve with cold meat or as a substitute for capers.

Red Cabbage

Choose firm solid hearts of a good colour. Cut into four
and remove the stalk, then shred downwards in thin slices.
Put the shredded cabbage on a big dish and layer well
with salt. Leave for 24 hours. Drain off the brine and pack
into jars. Have ready a spiced vinegar and pour into the

jars. Make sure that the cabbage is well covered. Tie down securely.

Kilner jars are good for storing red cabbage.

This pickle may be used after one week. Do not keep it more than 2-3 months as it will lose its crispness.

Cucumber Pickle – Sour

3-4 cucumbers: salt or brine: spiced vinegar.

Peel cucumbers with a potato peeler, cut into four and then across into 2 inch lengths. Sprinkle with salt or soak in brine for 24 hours.

Drain well, do not wash, and pack upright into jars. Fill to the top with hot spiced vinegar and screw down. Use after a week in pickle.

A small capsicum or chilli may be put into each jar if a hot pickle is liked.

Ripe Tomato Pickle

(A useful pickle when there is a glut of tomatoes.)

6 lb ripe, firm tomatoes: brine or salt: 2 lb brown sugar: 2 cloves of garlic: 1 quart vinegar: 2 blades mace: 2 sticks cinnamon: 1 oz allspice (Pimento).

Wipe and cut the tomatoes into thick slices, put into a crock and cover with brine or layer well with dry salt. Leave 24 hours. Then drain well.

Put sugar, garlic and vinegar together. Bring to the boil in a preserving pan, add the spices tied together in a piece of muslin. Add the tomatoes, reboil and simmer 2 minutes. Remove them carefully with a slice and pack them in layers in clean dry jars.

Boil the syrup and spices together until the syrup is thick when tested, as for a jam.

Pour into the jars and cover closely when cold.

For the brine, take ½ lb block salt to 2 quarts water. Allow to dissolve before using.

Pickled Onions

2 quarts peeled 'pickling' or silverskin onions: ½ cupful salt: 2 oz mixed pickling spice tied in a muslin bag: 1 quart good malt vinegar, brown or white.

To peel the onions, slice off the root and as little as possible of the crown. Scald with boiling water, drain after one minute, put into cold water and peel.

Put the onions into a bowl; sprinkle over the salt and stand overnight. Next day, rinse well and dry.

Boil the vinegar, sugar and spices together for five minutes. Throw in the onions and re-boil. Pack them into glass pickle jars; and cover well with the vinegar.

When cold screw on the lids or cover with parchment.

Pickled Walnuts

Walnuts for pickling must be picked before July for preference, or they become woody. It is best to wear rubber gloves to pick the walnuts with as they stain very badly and it is impossible to remove the stains.

Young green walnuts: salt, water, malt vinegar: peppercorns: allspice: root ginger.

Prick the walnuts all over with a long packing or carpet needle. Cover with brine – 6 oz salt to each quart of water. Leave in brine 5-6 days, then drain, cover with fresh brine and leave for another week. Drain and place on a tray in a sunny place, turning occasionally. When the walnuts are dry and black, pack them into jars and cover with spiced vinegar.

Allow 1 oz peppercorns, 1 oz allspice, $\frac{3}{4}$ oz root ginger, to each quart of vinegar. Bruise the spices, put in a muslin bag and boil in the vinegar for 10 minutes. Allow vinegar to cool. Remove spices. Cover walnuts and tie down. These will be ready to use in 6-8 weeks.

Pickled Mushrooms

Mushrooms, vinegar spiced with 3 blades of bruised mace to each quart: $\frac{1}{2}$ oz peppercorns, bruised.

Place the spices in a muslin bag, in a pan with the vinegar. Bring to boiling point with the lid on the pan and immediately set aside and allow to infuse 2-3 hours. Peel the mushrooms. Cut the stalks level with the caps, put into a pan. Sprinkle lightly with salt. Cook gently, shaking well till the juice flows. Continue to cook until the juice has evaporated. Cover with the spiced vinegar and simmer 2-3 minutes. Put carefully into jars and seal when cold.

Pickled Mushrooms – Simple

Rub small button mushrooms with salt and a little red pepper and place in a saucepan over very low heat. Shake as the moisture runs out of them so that they do not burn. Cover with good mild vinegar and simmer very gently until they are tender. Put into jars and tie down when cold.

Sweet Cucumber Pickle (1)

A pickle to make either with the hot-house or out-door cucumber when they are plentiful.

Sound cucumbers: alum water made with 1 dessert-spoon of powdered alum to each quart of water

Syrup made with 2 lb sugar, 1 pint vinegar and 2 table-spoons each of whole cloves and stick cinnamon tied together in a piece of muslin.

Pare the cucumbers thinly and if very large cut into quarters lengthways and then into 2 to 3 inch pieces. If medium or small, halve and cut across in the same way. Cover with the alum water and bring slowly to the boil. Then drain and chill the cucumber in ice water.

Have the syrup ready with all the ingredients boiled together for 5 minutes. Add the cucumbers and simmer for 10 minutes. Turn all into an earthenware crock or bowl. Leave till next day. On three successive days, drain off syrup, boil hard for one minute and then pour over the cucumbers. On the last day, pack the pieces carefully into jars and fill up with the boiling syrup.

Tie down when cold.

Sweet Cucumber Pickle (2)

3 lb ridge cucumbers, weighed when peeled and sliced: 1 lb medium sized onions, finely sliced: 2 green peppers, halved, the seeds removed and shredded: about 1½ oz salt.

Pickle: 10 oz brown or white sugar: 1½ oz mustard seed: 1 teaspoonful celery seed: 1 teaspoonful turmeric: ½ teaspoonful ground mace: 1 pint white malt or white wine vinegar.

Put the vegetables in layers in a bowl, sprinkling well with the salt. Cover and leave 2-3 hours. Drain, rinse with cold water and drain again. Meantime, put all the pickle ingredients together into a pan. Bring to the boil and boil two minutes. Add the drained vegetables and bring again to boiling point, stirring well from time to time. Turn into jars, cover with waxed paper and then with cellophane or parchment.

Make sure that the vegetables really boil, before potting down.

Sweet Cucumber Pickle (3)

6 ripe ridge cucumbers: 2-3 pints water: 2-3 heaped tablespoons salt: 1 lb seeded raisins; 3 lemons: 4 oz soft brown sugar.

Syrup: 2 lb soft brown sugar: 1 quart white distilled vinegar: 2 teaspoons allspice: 6 cloves: 1 inch cinnamon stick.

Split the cucumber lengthways; do not peel but scrape out the seeds. Tie the pieces of cucumber together, lay them in the strong salt water and leave for three days. Remove and soak in clear water for one day.

Cut the lemons in half, remove any pips and then put through the mincer or chop with the raisins. Place this mixture in a pan with the 4 oz brown sugar and simmer together until thick.

Drain the cucumber, fill with raisin and lemon mixture, tie again quite firmly and pack in an earthenware jar and put with them the spices tied together in a small muslin bag.

Dissolve the 2 lb brown sugar in the vinegar and boil for 10 minutes. Pour this hot syrup over the cucumbers and leave for 5 days. Drain off the syrup, heat to boiling point, pour over the cucumber and leave again for 5 days. Repeat this process and leave a further 5 days, when the cucumber will be ready for use.

Keeps well.

Sweet Green Tomato Pickle

3 lb small, even-sized green tomatoes: 1¼ pints water:

$\frac{1}{2}$ pint good vinegar: 1 level dessertspoon of salt.

Pickle: $\frac{1}{4}$ pint wine vinegar: 1 pint water: 2 lb sugar: 1 fresh chilli or 2 dried: 10 cloves.

Wipe tomatoes and prick all over with a silver fork. Boil water, salt and vinegar together, pour over tomatoes and leave for 24 hours. Prepare pickle, boil the vinegar, water and sugar together with the spices tied in a piece of muslin. When a clear syrup appears (after about 5-7 minutes boiling), put in the tomatoes, well drained from the vinegar water, and simmer until tender. Remove carefully and put into wide-necked glass jars.

Remove spices and boil syrup 7-10 minutes longer, pour over the tomatoes and cover well.

This pickle is best preserved in bottling jars.

Sweet Pickled Onions

Small pickling onions: tarragon: mixed spice: wine vinegar: salt: green or red pepper: white sugar.

Put the onions on a large plate and cover well with salt. Leave for 12 hours, wipe all the moisture off and pack into jars with sprigs of tarragon and a piece of red or green pepper. Add 1 teaspoon of whole mixed spice to every 1 lb jar. Boil sugar in the proportion of 6 oz white sugar to every $1\frac{1}{4}$ pints wine vinegar, or a little more sugar if the vinegar is unusually strong. Pour into the jars and tie down at once.

Spiced Apples

3 lb apples, weighed when peeled, quartered and cored: 4 lb preserving or granulated sugar: 2 pints wine or white malt vinegar: 1 oz stick cinnamon: $\frac{1}{2}$ oz cloves.

Dissolve sugar in the vinegar, bring to the boil. Add

spices tied in a muslin bag and the apples. Simmer very gently until the apples are tender but not broken. Then remove them carefully and pack into clean jars.

Boil down the syrup until thick and pour into the jars to cover the apples. Cover or screw down the tops when cold. Keep 6-8 weeks before using.

It is advisable to remove the spices before boiling down the syrup. The spices may be varied to taste and, if a sweet hot pickle is liked, include fresh or dried chillis. Tie these in the bag and remove when the flavour is hot enough for your liking.

Choose apples that will keep firm when cooked.

Spiced Rhubarb

Rhubarb: ½ lb sugar and 1 quart white distilled vinegar to every 2 lb of fruit: 1 tablespoon mixed pickling spice: ½ inch piece of stick cinnamon.

Wipe the rhubarb, cut into pieces about 1½ inches long and place in an earthenware basin with the sugar. Boil the spices with the vinegar, pour over the fruit and sugar and leave for 24 hours. Strain off the liquid, boil it for 5 minutes, pour over the fruit and again leave to stand until the next day. Strain once more and boil the liquid for 10 minutes. Now add the fruit to the liquid and heat together very carefully. Do not let the fruit boil. Turn into an earthenware bowl and when quite cold put into small pots and tie down securely.

Spiced Plums

Choose ripe, even-sized, sound plums. Make sure they are dry before pricking them well with an orange stick. Pack them closely into clean, dry jars with layers of black currant leaves, about 4 or 5 to a pound jar. Insert a stick of cinnamon and a clove or two in each jar. Put a black currant leaf on top.

Make a syrup with vinegar and sugar, allowing 1 pint of vinegar to ¾ lb sugar. Boil together for 4-5 minutes, then pour it boiling over the plums.

Cover closely when cold. These are best preserved in bottling jars.

Leave for two months before using.

Damson Pickle

4 quarts damsons: 4 lb cane or preserving sugar: ¾ pint good vinegar: 1 stick cinnamon: 6 cloves.

Wash and prick damsons with a silver fork. Put them in alternate layers in the preserving pan, add the vinegar. Bring slowly to the boil, shaking the pan occasionally to bring the liquid up over the damsons.

Simmer for 5 minutes, then lift the damsons from the syrup with a perforated ladle or fish slice, and lay them on flat dishes.

Add the spices to the syrup and boil for a further 15-20 minutes or until thick and syrupy. Put the fruit carefully into glass jars, strain the syrup and pour it on boiling hot.

Cover when cold.

Sweet Pickled Pears

7 lb pears: 3 lb sugar: ½ teaspoon stick cinnamon, broken in pieces: 1 pint cider or wine vinegar: ½ teaspoon whole cloves.

Any good cooking pear may be used. Peel, slice and core large pears, leave small pears whole. Put the spices in a muslin bag, add to vinegar and sugar and bring to the boil. Put in the pears and cook them slowly until they are tender and look clear. Remove them with a spoon and put them into sterilised jars. Boil the syrup until it becomes thick, pour over the pears and seal.

Note: When boiling down syrup to pour over spiced fruits, it is advisable to test as for jellies, i.e. to get a right consistency of the syrup when cold. Generally speaking, this should be as thick as cream.

Pickled or Spiced Cherries

4 lb cherries, Morellos or May Duke: 2 lb sugar: 1 pint white malt or white wine vinegar.

Spices: 3 roots ginger, bruised: 1 stick cinnamon: 3-4 cloves: rind of $\frac{1}{2}$ lemon.

Stone cherries, put into a jar, cover, stand in hot water and cook gently on stove top or in oven until barely tender. In the meantime, simmer together vinegar, sugar, and spices tied in a muslin bag. Add juice from cherries and pack into small jars. Remove spices and boil hard until a thick syrup appears. Pour this over the cherries and tie or screw down the lids at once. These are best potted in small screw-top honey jars.

Spiced Crabapples

3 lb good sound crabapples: 2 lb sugar: 1 pint vinegar.

Spices: 1 root ginger, well bruised: pared rind of half a lemon: 2 inch piece stick cinnamon: 2-3 cloves: 1 teaspoon whole pimento (allspice).

Wash and pick over the crabs. Put the vinegar and sugar into a saucepan, heat slowly, stirring occasionally. Add spices, tied in a small muslin bag, to the fruit. Cover pan and cook very gently until just tender. Then remove fruit carefully with a perforated spoon and pack into small to medium-sized jars. Remove spices and strain liquid. Now boil the liquid in the pan, uncovered, until it is the consistency of syrup. Pour hot into the jars to cover the fruit by ½ inch. Seal tightly and store in a cool dark place for 6 weeks before using.

Sweet Pickled Oranges

12 fine large oranges: 1¾ pints white wine vinegar: 2¾ lb preserving or loaf sugar: 1½ sticks cinnamon: ½ oz cloves: 6 blades mace.

Slice oranges about ¼ inch thick, lay them in a pan and just cover with water. Simmer, with the pan covered, until the peel is tender, about 1½ hours. Put the vinegar, sugar and spices into a pan and boil well together for a few minutes. Drain the oranges carefully, reserving the liquor. Lay half of them in the syrup, making sure that it covers them. Put the lid on the pan and simmer 30-40 minutes until the oranges turn clear. Lift out into a shallow dish, put the rest of the oranges into the pan and if not covered by the syrup add a little of the reserved orange liquor. Cook as before. Turn all into the bowl, cover and leave overnight. If necessary, pour off the syrup and boil until thick. Add the slices and reboil. Arrange carefully in warm jars, tie down. If the syrup is thick and well reduced, merely heat slowly to boiling point with the oranges, then pot and tie down.

Should there not be sufficient syrup to cover, make fresh syrup in the above proportion of vinegar to sugar, boil until thick, and fill up the jars. The spices may be left in the syrup or put into a muslin bag and removed before potting. Make sure the oranges are kept covered by the syrup during storage. If they become uncovered by evaporation, they will discolour.

Spiced Peaches

2 pints white wine or white distilled vinegar: 1 oz cloves: ½ oz cinnamon stick and 1 oz allspice (tied in muslin): 4 lb sugar: 7 lb peaches.

Bring vinegar, containing spices, to boiling point. Peel the peaches. The golden yellow, thick skinned imported peaches, called 'Hale' or 'Cling' are best for this, and these must be scalded for peeling. If garden peaches are used they should not be too ripe and may also need scalding. Large peaches should be split and stoned. Drop the peaches into the boiling liquid. Cook till tender, taking care to see that they are cooked through. Lift out into jars. Boil syrup until thick and pour over the peaches. Tie down. Treat apricots in the same way, either whole or split.

Pickled Grapes

Black or green grapes may be used for this pickle.

Make sure the grapes are perfectly sound.

Divide them into small bunches, and pack into clean, dry jars with a good sprinkling of dry mustard put in in layers.

Make a thin syrup with ¼ lb sugar to 1 pint of water, flavour it with cinnamon and cloves and allow to cool. Strain into the jars and tie down closely.

Leave three months to mature.

Pickled Dried Figs

1 lb dried figs: ½ pint wine vinegar: 4 oz granulated sugar: 1 inch piece stick cinnamon: 4 cloves: 3 allspice berries.

Cover the figs with water and simmer for 15 minutes. Drain off the water, add the vinegar, sugar and spices and cook together a further 15 minutes.

Pack into hot sterilised jars and seal at once.

Melon Pickle

1 lb melon (weighed after preparation): 1 lb loaf sugar: ½ gill white distilled vinegar: 20 cloves.

Peel the melon, remove the seeds and cut into chunky pieces. Dissolve the sugar in the vinegar, bring to the boil and pour over the prepared fruit. Leave to stand 10-15 minutes. Drain off the liquid and bring to the boil. Add the fruit to the pan and boil gently for about 3 hours. Pour into warm dry jars and cover when cold.

Green Tomato Pickle

7 lb green tomatoes: 3 large onions: 1 quart water: 3 pints white distilled vinegar: 1 lb sugar: ½ oz cloves: ½ oz whole root ginger: ½ oz allspice: ½ oz mustard seed: a good pinch of cayenne.

Slice the tomatoes and onions, sprinkle well with salt and leave to stand overnight. The next day, drain and place in a stewpan with the water and 1 pint of the vinegar. Boil for ½ hour, drain again, throwing away the water and vinegar. Cover the tomatoes and onions with the remaining 2 pints vinegar, add the sugar and cayenne pepper and the spices tied in a piece of muslin. Stir over gentle heat until the sugar dissolves and then boil for ½ hour. Remove the bag of spices, pour into warm, dry jars and tie down when cold.

Gooseberry Pickle

1 quart unripe gooseberries: $\frac{1}{2}$ lb brown sugar: salt: 1 quart white wine vinegar: $\frac{1}{4}$ lb mustard seed: 6 oz garlic: $\frac{3}{4}$ lb stoned raisins: $\frac{1}{2}$ oz cayenne pepper.

Place the gooseberries in a stewpan with the sugar and salt and half the vinegar, and stir over gentle heat until the sugar dissolves, then bring to the boil and cook until the gooseberries are tender.

Bruise the mustard seeds, chop and crush the garlic and mix with the raisins and cayenne. Pour over the boiling gooseberries and, finally, add the remaining 1 pint of cold vinegar. Store in kilner jars for at least 6 months before using.

★

CHAPTER IV

Chutneys, Relishes and Ketchups

THERE ARE no special rules for these. Generally speaking the main ingredients are salted overnight, or for some hours before being simmered with spices and vinegar. It is advisable to cover the jars with a specially prepared paper which helps to prevent evaporation of the contents. Preparations containing vinegar are liable to dry out and so chutnies, pickles, etc., have to be well sealed.

For details of the best kind of vinegar to use, the type of pan etc., see the introduction to the pickle chapter.

Apple and Tomato Chutney

2 lb apples: 2 lb tomatoes (red): 2 onions: 1 pint vinegar: 1 teaspoon peppercorns: 1 level dessertspoon ground ginger: ½ lb brown sugar.

Peel, core and slice the apples, tomatoes and onions. Put them in a large bowl, pour over them the vinegar, add the peppercorns and ginger, cover and leave until the next day. Turn all together into a preserving pan, stir frequently and simmer until tender. Pour into jars and cover closely when cold.

Apple and Raisin Chutney – American Recipe

2 quarts of apples, cut in small pieces for measuring: 2 lb granulated sugar: 2 cups seeded raisins: ½ cup of strong vinegar: rind of 2 oranges finely chopped, and the juice:

$\frac{1}{8}$ teaspoon ground cloves: 1 cup finely chopped nuts (walnuts, almonds, etc.).

Simmer all ingredients together until apples and nuts are tender. Turn into warm jars and tie down.

This is a fairly sweet chutney.

An American cup is 8 liquid ounces.

Apricot Chutney with Fresh Apricots

5 lb apricots, weighed when split and stoned: 3 lb onions: 1 lb raisins stoned: 2 lb brown sugar: 2 tablespoons mustard seed: 1 level teaspoon chilli powder: 2 dessertspoons salt: 2 pints malt vinegar: grated rind and juice of 2 oranges: 1 teaspoon cinnamon: 2 level teaspoons turmeric: 4 oz shelled walnuts: grated rind and juice of 2 lemons.

Put all ingredients into preserving pan with the exception of the walnuts. Simmer until soft and pulpy, add walnuts and pot.

Date and Dried Apricot Chutney

2 lb dates: 1 lb dried apricots: $\frac{1}{2}$ lb preserved ginger: 3 cloves of garlic: 1 lb sultanas or seedless raisins: 1 lb sugar: 4 tablespoons salt: white malt vinegar to cover.

Soak apricots 24 hours, stone dates. Crush garlic with a little of the salt, chop ginger. Cook all ingredients together till rich and pulpy – about 2 hours. Pot.

Hot Chutney

3 lb apples: 1 quart wine vinegar: 2 oz garlic: $\frac{1}{2}$ lb green ginger: $\frac{1}{2}$ lb seedless raisins: $\frac{1}{2}$ lb fresh chillis: $\frac{1}{2}$ lb mustard seed: 1 lb brown sugar: 1 pint water: 4 oz salt.

Peel and cut up apples and boil in half the vinegar or sufficient to cover. Crush the garlic with a little salt, grate the green ginger, chop raisins and chillis (or they can be put through a mincing machine). Crush the mustard seed with a rolling pin or in a mortar.

Make a syrup with the sugar and one pint of water. Place cooked apples in a bowl, sprinkle with salt and remaining ingredients and add the syrup, the rest of the vinegar, and that from the apples. Bottle and seal with a layer of paraffin wax and a cork or jam cover.

This is best after keeping for a few months, and is most useful for devils, barbecues and so on.

Ginger and Apple Chutney

2 dozen large apples: 1 lb sultanas: 2 lb Demerara sugar: 3 oz mustard seed: 1 fresh chilli or 4 dried: 1 level dessert-spoon turmeric: 1½ oz ground ginger: 1 lb Spanish onions cut in half and thinly sliced: 4 cloves garlic, peeled and crushed with a little salt: 1½ pints vinegar.

Pare, core and slice the apples. Cut fresh chilli into rings. Put all together into a large pan. Simmer gently 1½-2 hours until thoroughly cooked and pulpy. Leave overnight.

Orange and Apple Chutney

4 lb apples: 1 lb seedless raisins or sultanas: 2 oranges or 3 tangerines: 2 lb sugar, including some lump if the zest of the orange is taken: 1½ pints vinegar: pinch of ground cloves: ½ lb chopped walnuts.

Peel, core and chop the apples. Chop raisins. Remove zest of the oranges with a few lumps of sugar, or cut thinly pared rind finely. Cook apples, raisins, nuts and spice with 1 pint of vinegar and add the cloves tied in muslin. Simmer in a covered pan until thoroughly cooked. Pour remaining vinegar over the sugar and put in a warm place until sugar has dissolved. When the fruits are cooked, add the sugar, vinegar and orange juice and rind (or zest) and cook in an uncovered pan until thick.

Marrow Chutney

4 lb marrows: ½ lb pickling onions: 6 cloves: 1½ lb loaf sugar: ½ oz turmeric: 9 chillis: 1½ oz ground ginger: 1½ oz mustard: 2 quarts vinegar: salt.

Cut the marrow into small squares (about ½ inch), lay on a dish and shake some salt over it and leave overnight. Drain. Boil remaining ingredients for 10 minutes, then add the marrow and boil for half an hour or until tender and put into jars.

Date Chutney

Use for sandwiches with cheese. It is useful to make around Christmas time when dates are good and plentiful; it is a chutney that can be eaten soon after it is made.

2 lb dates, stoned: 1-2 dried chillis: 1 lb onions finely chopped: 4 cloves, garlic, crushed to a cream with a little salt: ½ lb sultanas: 1 teaspoonful salt: 1 level teaspoonful ground ginger: ½ teaspoonful pepper: 1½ pints vinegar.

Cut dates and chilli into small pieces. Put into a pan with the onions, garlic, sultanas, seasonings and vinegar. Simmer gently until the mixture is rich and thick, about 1-1½ hours. Turn into small pots.

Plum Chutney

3 lb plums: 1 lb soft brown sugar: ¾ pint vinegar: 1 oz salt: 1½ tablespoons allspice: 1 tablespoon ground ginger: 1 dessertspoon mustard seed: 6 chillies: 10 cloves.

Wash and stone plums, put into a pan with ginger. Crush mustard seed and put with rest of spices in a muslin bag. Tie bag and put in pan. Add salt and ½ pint of vinegar. Put on lid, simmer gently till soft (about 3 hours). Cover sugar in basin with rest of vinegar, leave to dissolve and add to plums when cooked. Bring to boil and continue to boil gently until chutney is thick (another 2 hours). Pour into hot jars and cover at once. Leave 4-5 weeks before use.

Green Tomato Chutney

9 lb tomatoes: 4 green or red peppers chopped: 2½ lb onions, sliced: 2½ lb apples, weighed when cored and sliced: 1¼ lb sultanas: 2 oz mustard seed: 2 oz salt: 1 large root of ginger, well bruised: ½ teaspoon cayenne: 2½ lb brown sugar: 3 pints good vinegar.

Place all ingredients in a preserving pan. Simmer slowly 2-3 hours or until thoroughly cooked. Remove ginger before putting into pots.

Red Tomato and Pepper Chutney

5 lb good ripe tomatoes: 4 large yellow or green peppers, seeded, cut in small shreds and blanched: 2 large onions: 1 oz salt: ½ oz mustard seed: 1½ pints good vinegar: (½ oz celery seed, ½ oz whole allspice: ½ oz root ginger: ¼ oz cloves: 2-3 cummin seeds, bruised: all tied in a muslin bag): 1 lb brown sugar.

Scald and peel the tomatoes, cut in half, remove the hard piece of stalk and squeeze gently to remove the seeds and water. Strain these and put the juice with the halves of the tomatoes into a preserving pan. Add the peppers, onions, salt and mustard seed, and allow to simmer gently for 20-25 minutes. Meanwhile, boil the remaining spices with the vinegar for the same time with the lid on the pan; remove the bag and add the vinegar to the tomatoes with the sugar. Continue to boil gently 1-2 hours, stirring occasionally, and then more frequently. If the chutney is to be well spiced, put in the muslin bag again when the vinegar is added and remove it as the mixture thickens. When it is fairly thick, stir into an earthenware bowl. Leave overnight, pot and tie down.

Pear Chutney with Windfall Pears

3½ lb windfall pears, weighed when peeled, cored and quartered: 1 lb onion, sliced and chopped: ¾ lb raisins, stoned and chopped: ½ lb apples, weighed when peeled, cored and sliced: ¼ lb sliced stem ginger: 3 cloves of garlic crushed with a little salt: 1 oz salt: grated rind and juice of 1 small lemon: ¾ lb brown sugar: 4 dried capsicums: 3-4 cloves tied in a muslin bag: 1 quart of good vinegar.

Put the pears into an earthenware crock or bowl with the onions, raisins, apples, ginger, garlic, salt and lemon. Put sugar, spices and vinegar into a pan and boil 3-4 minutes. Pour over the contents of the bowl and leave 12 hours. Boil gently 3-4 hours or until dark and rich. Remove bag of cloves half-way through the boiling or when you have sufficient flavour.

Tomato Chutney

3 doz large fine ripe tomatoes: 6 large onions, cut in half and thinly sliced: 6 green peppers, cut in half and thinly sliced: 2½ pints vinegar: 2 oz salt: 8 oz brown sugar: grated rind and juice of 2 lemons: ½ teaspoon each ground ginger, pepper and mace.

Scald and peel the tomatoes, cut into quarters, removing most of the seeds and water. Strain these and put into a large pan with the tomatoes. Add remaining ingredients and boil gently 1-2 hours. Turn into clean, dry jars. Tie or screw down.

Note: Apples may be used in place of peppers.

Sweet Pepper Chutney

8 large red peppers: 8 large green peppers: 8 medium sized onions: 1 oz salt: 12 oz granulated sugar: 1 heaped teaspoon mustard seed: 1½ pints white malt or white wine vinegar.

Split the peppers and remove the seeds. Mince them or chop finely. Chop the onions. Put altogether into a bowl and pour on boiling water to cover well. Drain at once, turn into a pan, cover with cold water and bring to the boil. Drain again. Now put the salt, sugar, seed and vinegar into the pan, bring to the boil and add the pepper mixture, making sure it is thoroughly drained from the blanching. Re-boil and simmer about 20-30 minutes. Turn into small warm jars and tie down. This chutney can be used at once if wished.

Red Pepper Marmalade

6 red peppers: 6 oranges: 1 lemon: granulated sugar.

Cut oranges into thin slices, add the juice and grated rind of the lemon, barely cover with water and simmer until tender. Add the sliced pepper and measure the fruit. To each pint of fruit add ¾ lb granulated sugar. Dissolve over gentle heat and then boil rapidly until the marmalade is stiff enough to set when tested. Pour into warm dry jars.

Mint Relish

1 lb sugar: good ¾ pint of vinegar: 2 oz mint leaves: 12 oz stoned raisins: ½ lb onions: ½ lb tomatoes: 2 teaspoons salt: 1 level teaspoon mustard: 1 lb cooking apples.

Heat vinegar, add sugar, salt and mustard. Put the other ingredients through the mincer, add to the vinegar, etc., boil 20 minutes, pot and seal.

Mushroom Ketchup

Weigh some dry open mushrooms and allow 1½ oz salt to every pound. Break up the mushrooms and put in layers, sprinkled with salt in a stone jar and leave 3-4 days. Stir and press from time to time. At the end of this time press well, cover the jar and put it in a cool oven for 2-3 hours. Strain through a fine nylon sieve. Gently press to extract all the juice. To each quart of liquor allow:

½ oz allspice: ½ root ginger: 2 blades of mace: pinch of cayenne (optional): 1 shallot, chopped.

Put all into a muslin bag. Put the liquid and spice into a pan and simmer 2-3 hours until well reduced. Strain, put into proper sterilising bottles and sterilise 15 minutes. This is a precautionary measure. Some red wine in the proportion of a quarter of the quantity of mushroom liquor may be added and boiled with the liquid, or a few drops of brandy may be added to each pint.

Gooseberry Ketchup

Put 2 quarts of gooseberries, 2 cups of vinegar, 3 lb brown sugar and a dessertspoonful each of cinnamon, cloves and allspice in an aluminium or enamel pan. Cook slowly for 2 hours, being careful that it does not burn. Put into wide mouthed bottles and seal down tightly.

Very good with cold meat.

Gooseberry Relish

2 lb gooseberries: 12 oz raisins: 1 lb onions: ½ lb brown sugar: level tablespoon mustard: 1 tablespoon ground ginger: 2 level tablespoons salt: ¼ teaspoon cayenne: 1 level teaspoon turmeric: 1 pint vinegar.

Pick over, wash and drain gooseberries; add raisins (from which seeds have been removed) and peeled and sliced onion. Chop or put through a mincer, put in preserving kettle and add sugar, mustard, ginger, salt, cayenne and turmeric. Pour over vinegar, bring slowly to the boil, and simmer 45 minutes. Rub through a coarse sieve, fill bottles with mixture and seal.

The consistency of this relish is that of a thick sauce.

Plum Sauce

4½ lb red plums: 6 lb onions: 2 quarts vinegar: 4 oz salt: 1 lb sugar: 2 oz mustard: ½ lb sultanas: ½ oz chillies: 1 oz whole ginger: 1 oz allspice: ½ oz turmeric: 1 nutmeg ground.

Wipe and stone the plums. Slice the onions. Put the plums, onions, sultanas, chillies and crushed ginger into half the vinegar. Bring to the boil and simmer for thirty minutes. Sieve and put back into the pan with the sugar, salt, nutmeg, allspice and turmeric. Add the remaining vinegar and simmer for 30 minutes. Bottle when cold.

Hot Tomato Sauce

(An especially good sauce, which also improves with keeping.)

18 large tomatoes: 9 lb medium apples: 9 fresh chillies, preferably the red kind (dried chillies may be substituted, but double the quantity must be used): 4 medium-sized onions: 3 tablespoons salt: $1\frac{1}{2}$ level teaspoons each ground cloves and allspice: 3 level teaspoons each celery seed and dry mustard: 3 cloves of garlic, crushed: 1 lb, 2 oz sugar: $1\frac{1}{2}$ pints vinegar.

Peel and quarter the tomatoes, sprinkle with the salt. Leave an hour or two. In the meantime, peel, quarter and core the apples, and then chop them. Mince or chop chillies. Chop onions. Add the spices and sugar to the vinegar and bring to the boil. Add the tomatoes, apples, chillies and onions. Simmer gently for about $1\frac{1}{2}$-2 hours or until clear and thick. Stir frequently, as the sauce becomes thick, to prevent its catching fire.

Cool slightly before pouring into bottles. As an alternative, the sauce may be sieved after about an hour and a half's simmering and then returned to the cleaned pan to finish.

Tomato Sauce

A useful sauce that improves with keeping. Choose tomatoes especially ripe and red.

6 lb tomatoes: 2 level tablespoons salt: 2 tart cooking apples: $\frac{3}{4}$ lb onions: 6 oz sugar: $\frac{3}{4}$ pint vinegar: 1 dessertspoon pepper: 1 level teaspoon ground cloves: 1 level teaspoon ground mace.

Wipe and slice tomatoes, lay them on a dish and sprinkle them with the salt. Leave for about an hour. Wipe apples, quarter and core and chop roughly. Chop the onions. Put them both into the pan with the sugar, vinegar and spices. Bring to the boil, then add the tomatoes. Simmer *gently* for about 2 hours, by which time the mixture should be thoroughly pulpy and well flavoured. Pass through a sieve. Return to the cleaned pan and continue to simmer until fairly thick, probably for half to one hour. This depends on the juiciness of the tomatoes, but the sauce when cold must not be too thick to pour out of the bottles. When the mixture is the right consistency, cool slightly and pour off into sauce bottles. Screw down tightly and label when cold.

Tomato Purée

See also page 80.

To 8 lb of red ripe tomatoes take: 2 chopped onions: 2 cloves of garlic, crushed: half a dozen sprays of parsley: 2 sprigs thyme: 2 bay leaves: 2 level tablespoons salt and the same of sugar: 1 level teaspoon ground pepper.

Wash tomatoes, remove stalks and quarter. Put into a pan with the rest of the ingredients and bring slowly to the boil, crushing and bruising the tomatoes as much as possible. Simmer until tomatoes are very soft (about an hour). Push through a nylon sieve or, failing this, an aluminium strainer. Return to the cleaned pan and boil, stirring frequently, until very thick. Turn into warm *small* jars (small honey jars are suitable); screw down and sterilise 35-40 minutes. Label and store.

Green Tomato Chutney

3½ lb green tomatoes: 1 teaspoon mustard seed: 1 teaspoon ground ginger: 1 teaspoon ground allspice: 10 cloves: 1 onion: 1 quart vinegar: 1 lb brown sugar: 1 teaspoon salt.

Peel the tomatoes, cut in small pieces and put into a

pan with the vinegar, sugar and salt. Dissolve the sugar over gentle heat and then add the spices and finely chopped onion. Boil gently for about 1½-2 hours. Turn into an earthenware bowl and leave overnight. Stir well, fill into clean dry jars and tie down.

Red Tomato Chutney

2 lb ripe but firm tomatoes: 2 lb apples: 1 lb onions: ½ lb sultanas: 1 level teaspoon dry mustard and ground ginger: 1 level tablespoon salt: 1 lb brown sugar: 1 quart vinegar.

Scald and skin the tomatoes and cut into thick slices; wipe and core the apples and cut into small pieces; do not remove the peel. Place the prepared fruits into a pan with the finely chopped onions, the sultanas, sugar and seasonings; cover with the vinegar and cook slowly for about 2 hours. Pour into warm dry jars and tie down when cold.

Indian Chutney – Very Hot

1 lb moist brown sugar: ¼ pint water: ½ lb mustard seed: 2 oz garlic: ½ lb green ginger: ½ lb fresh chillies: ½ lb stoned raisins: 15 sour apples: 1 quart vinegar: ½ lb salt.

Make the sugar into a syrup with ¼ pint water. Wash and dry the seed and bruise it. Thinly slice the garlic, ginger and chillies.

Peel, quarter and core the apples, simmer till tender in enough of the vinegar to moisten them well. When they are cold, lay them in a shallow bowl. Sprinkle first with the salt, then with mustard seed, garlic, chillies, ginger and raisins. Mix with the syrup by degrees, stirring well and adding the vinegar from the apples and any remaining vinegar. When well mixed, turn into screw-top jars to seal well.

Mushroom Ketchup

To make when field mushrooms are cheap!

10 lb mushrooms: 4 level tablespoons salt: 1 small onion: 1 teaspoon ground allspice and cloves: 1 teaspoon grated horseradish: ¼ teaspoon cayenne: ½ pint vinegar.

Wash the mushrooms quickly, skin and trim the stalks, and chop them coarsely. Put into a large pan, sprinkling them with the salt and leave to stand overnight. The next morning, add the remaining ingredients to the pan, bring to the boil, and simmer for half an hour. Pass through a fine sieve or 'mouli' or purée in the electric blender. Return to the pan, bring to the boil and pour at once into hot sterliised jars and seal at once.

★

CHAPTER V

Bottling and Canning

BOTTLING

THERE IS nothing more satisfying to the housewife than to have a good store of bottled fruits put by for the winter. Fruit pies, flans and salads can thus be enjoyed during the more expensive months at an economic price.

The principle of preserving fruit by bottling depends upon, firstly, the destruction by heat of all the moulds and bacteria in the air, fruit, or water in the bottles and secondly, the exclusion of air during sterilisation and the complete sealing of the bottles by vacuum afterwards. Acid in the fruit keeps sterilisation and consequently acid fruits bottle the most satisfactorily.

When vegetables are being bottled a solution of lemon juice, salt and water is used for the same reason and also to destroy any soil bacteria when a pressure cooker is not available.

Equipment is simple and may be used year after year with only small replacements.

Two or three firms specialise in bottling apparatus, bottles, sterilisers and so on, and though make-shifts can be used, a more reliable and better result is obtained from using the proper equipment. Sterilising outfits are available complete with bottles, rings, clips, thermometer, etc., in varying sizes. These simplify the process for those who have had little experience in bottling, or who wish to undertake more. The number of jars can be added to from time to time according to the amount of bottling done.

There are two main types of jars or bottles – those with a glass lid and metal screw cap, and those with a metal lid and clip. Both types have rubber rings and are made in different sizes. The advantage of the latter type is that the neck of the jar also varies in size, which makes for ease and speed in packing. For example, a small-sized jar can have a wide neck so that the hand may be inserted.

All sterilisers should have a false bottom so that bottles do not come into contact with the direct heat, and a slot at the side or in the lid, for the thermometer. If a proper steriliser is not available, a bread bin or flour bin with a doubled piece of wire netting placed on the bottom, may be used.

An essential is that the water must come up to the neck of the bottles and therefore, if fair-sized bottles are used, the pan must be deep. For small-sized jars a fish kettle is useful.

There are two main methods of sterilising or bottling fruit, the hot water bath method and the oven method. Whichever method is chosen, the following rules must be observed:

1 Choose fruit that is perfectly sound, firm, barely ripe and without blemish. Grade, so that all the fruit in one bottle is approximately the same size.

2 Pack firmly into thoroughly clean jars that have been rinsed in cold water and left wet inside. Avoid crushing the fruit in any way. Fill to within ½ inch of the top, using a wooden packing spoon or the handle of a spoon.

3 Fill with water or syrup – this may be cold or boiling, according to the method followed. Make sure that all air bubbles disappear before you put on the lids. This can be helped by gently tapping the jar on the table or 'padding' the top of the liquid with a spoon. Both colour and flavour are improved if syrup is used. The syrup may vary in strength, according to the acidity of the fruit, from 1 lb

to 1 quart of water to 1½-2 lb to 1 quart of water. Too heavy a syrup may make some fruit rise in the bottles and, in the case of gooseberries, will toughen the skins.

Prepare the syrup by dissolving the sugar in the water over gentle heat and then bring to the boil.

Boil 2-3 minutes, then strain through muslin.

4 Soak rubber rings in cold water before use and renew every year. Discard any jar with a chip on rim or lid as it will never seal.

5 After sterilising, do not remove clips or screw bands for 48 hours; after this time, test for sealing before storing. The lids should be firm on the bottles. Replace screw bands, smearing lightly with a little salad oil. Do not screw down too tightly.

6 Store the bottles in a cool dry cupboard away from the light if the colour is to be preserved.

HOT WATER BATH METHOD

Here a special steriliser and thermometer simplifies the operation and makes for better results.

1 Pack the jars with the chosen fruit.

2 Fill to the brim with cold syrup or water; seal firmly with the rubber rings and caps. If screw bands, do not tighten.

3 Stand jars in steriliser or in a deep pan or container with a piece of wood or wire netting laid on the bottom. A bread or flour-bin answers well in an emergency.

4 Fill with cold water up to the neck of the jars.

5 Put in thermometer and heat *slowly* to correct temperature, which varies according to the kind of fruit. Allow 1½ hours for this. (See chart, p. 78).

6 If no thermometer is available bring water in pan to simmering point only, taking 1½ hours to do so. Maintain

at that temperature 6–15 minutes for soft fruit, 20 minutes for pears, and 30 minutes for tomatoes.

7 Lift jars out on to a wooden board or table and allow to cool; tighten screws slightly.

8 Test for sealing after 48 hours, by removing screw band or clip. The lids should be fast on the bottles.

This method gives the best results for colour, texture and flavour. Always use a thermometer if possible, otherwise the fruit is inclined to crack and rise unduly in the jar and the appearance is spoilt.

For a quicker version of this method:

1 Fill the jars, after packing them with the fruit, with boiling syrup or water; screw down lids or clips on the caps.

2 Set jars in steriliser or pan and pour in enough boiling water to cover the jars completely. Leave on the boil from 5–20 minutes.

This method is not to be recommended if the fruit is required whole and of good appearance, but the flavour is excellent.

OVEN METHOD A

1 Use special bottling jar with rubber rings, clips or screw tops.

2 Pack fruit in and fill to within ½ inch of the brim with cold syrup or water.

3 Put rings on with the lids, but do not clip or screw right down.

4 Stand jars in cool oven on a piece of thin wood or thick cardboard, taking care that they do not touch one another or the oven wall.

5 Oven temperature must be between 280°F and 340°F, Reg. ¼ and 3–4. Start at the cooler temperature and raise

to the higher if necessary (pears, apples, etc.).

6 Keep in oven 1½-3 hours, again according to the variety of fruit. When shrinkage occurs and there is a slight space at the bottom of the jar and bubbles appear on the fruit, the jars are ready to be lifted from the oven.

7 Take out one at a time and clip or screw down firmly.

8 To get a good result, heating must be slow and gradual.

OVEN METHOD B

1 Any large jam jars or bottles can be used.

2 Pack with fruit as before, and cover the jars with a small saucer or lid of some kind.

3 Heat in oven as before, very gradually, at temperature of 250° F.

4 After about an hour or less, when the fruit has shrunk slightly, remove jars from oven one at a time.

5 If fruit has well shrunk the jar may be filled up with fruit from another jar. Pour on boiling syrup or water at once to cover.

6 Immediately put on rings and lids (snap closure type) and clip down, or tie down securely with parchment or skin (Porosan).

EQUIPMENT FOR BOTTLING

A steriliser complete with false bottom, lid and thermometer.

Bottles or jars. The number and size of these will vary with the size of household and the amount and kind of fruit you wish to preserve. As a general rule, keep the smaller jars for soft fruit, such as raspberries or strawberries, and the bigger ones for pears, plums, apples, etc.

Bottle tongs. These are of great help in lifting out the

jars from the steriliser. The grips are covered with rubber and hold the bottle firmly.

Packing spoon. This is a long-handled, small-bowled spoon and is invaluable for packing in the fruit, vegetables, etc.

Serrated-edged knife, made of stainless steel – invaluable for cutting tomatoes, plums, apricots, etc.

Butter muslin for blanching.

PREPARATION OF FRUIT AND TEMPERATURE CHART

Preparation

Apples

Peel and core, cut into quarters or ⅛ths, or into rings ⅛ of an inch thick and dip into boiling water 2-3 minutes. Pack into jars in the usual way.

Sterilise at 165° F. and maintain temperature for 10 minutes.

Apricots

Usually left whole but may be halved if large as this fruit may be packed quite closely. Crack some stones and add the blanched kernels to the jars.

Sterilise at 165° F. and maintain temperature for 10 minutes.

Blackberries

Overlook carefully and, if they appear to contain maggots, soak for ½ hour in salt water to draw the grubs out. The berries should be large, juicy and quite ripe.

Sterilise at 165° F. and maintain temperature for 10 minutes.

Cherries

Choose Morello or the Red Acid varieties, not the black or whiteheart cherries. Remove the stalks and wash in cold

Sterilise at 190° F. and maintain temperature for

water. Add ¼ oz citric acid to every 1 gallon syrup or water.

10 minutes.

Currants
Remove from the stems and wash.

Sterilise at 180° F. and maintain temperature for 15 minutes.

Gooseberries
Top and tail and wash in cold water. Prick each berry several times with a needle to prevent the skin toughening. Flavour the syrup with one or two heads of elderflower tied in muslin.

Sterilise at 165° F. and maintain temperature for 10 minutes.

Peaches and Plums
Skin the peaches by covering with boiling water for 1 minute. Halve or cut in slices. Wash plums in cold water and halve if large.

Sterilise at 165° F. and maintain temperature for 10 minutes.

Pears
Halve the pears, remove the core and fibres up to the stem with a sharp-pointed teaspoon, peel and drop immediately into the hot syrup. Allow to cool completely before beginning sterilisation.

Sterilise at 190° F. and maintain temperature for 20 minutes.

Raspberries and Strawberries
If clean and dry, pick straight into bottles to prevent unnecessary crushing.

Sterilise at 165° F. and maintain temperature for 10 minutes.

Preparation

Quinces

Prepare as for pears.   Sterilise at 190°
F. and maintain
temperature for
20 minutes.

TOMATOES

Tomatoes may be bottled in various forms:
  (a) in their own juice;
  (b) whole in brine;
  (c) as a thin purée;
  (d) as juice.

(a) *Solid Pack, or Tomatoes in their own juice*
  1 Blanch the tomatoes by dipping into boiling water for
     10 seconds, and then plunging into cold water before
     removing their skins. Pack the fruit into the jars very
     tightly, leaving no air spaces, halving or quartering the
     fruit if large, and adding ¼ oz salt and 1 teaspoonful
     sugar to each 2 lb tomatoes.
  2 Fix the rubber bands, put on lids, bands or clips and
     place in the steriliser. Take 1½ hours to reach simmering
     point and maintain this temperature for a further ½
     hour.

(b) *Whole Tomatoes in Brine*
  1 Skin the tomatoes in the usual way and preserve, using
     either the water bath or the oven method. In each case
     the liquid used is a brine solution made from ½ oz salt
     to 1 quart of water.

(c) *Tomato Purée*
  1 Wash the tomatoes, cut in half and cook *gently* in a
     covered pan until soft.

80

2 Rub through a hair or nylon sieve, reheat, adding sugar and salt to taste, bring to the boil and pour into hot clean preserving jars and seal immediately.

3 Place the jars in a pan of hot water, bring slowly to boiling point and continue boiling for 10 minu' :s.

(d) *Tomato Juice*

1 Prepare the tomatoes in the same way as for the purée and add to each quart of sieved tomato pulp $\frac{1}{2}$ pint water, 1 oz sugar, 1 teaspoonful salt and freshly ground black pepper.

2 Reheat, pot and sterilise in the same way as the purée.

BOTTLING VEGETABLES

Vegetables must be bottled in a different way from fruits (this also applies to canning), because being low in acidity, they need a greater temperature than that of boiling water to sterilise them effectively (i.e. a pressure cooker). Alternatively, an acid brine solution, sometimes known as the lemon-juice method, may be used; this obviates the use of the pressure cooker. Vegetables insufficiently sterilised can be dangerous and the use of a pressure cooker is to be recommended. The acid-brine method or a water bath method is, however, satisfactory, provided every detail is carried out correctly and with care.

The most popul. vegetables for home bottling are peas and broad and French beans. These should be freshly picked from the garden and bottled the same day. This is most important as bacteria are more difficult to kill on stale vegetables. All vegetables must first be blanched as a preliminary sterilisation, and this process must not be omitted. It also 'brings up' the colour and makes the vegetables easier to pack.

1 Have ready a pan of sufficient boiling water to cover the vegetables being blanched.

2 Put the prepared vegetables into a piece of muslin or salad basket.

3 Plunge the muslin bag or salad basket into the boiling water and leave for 3 minutes for peas and broad beans, and 5 minutes for French beans.

4 Drain and pack at once into hot jars. Do not pack down tightly. Leave a space of about ¾ to 1 inch from the top of the jar. Pour on the boiling liquid required in the method being followed, and put on the lids. If screw-top jars are being used, leave bands half unscrewed but clip down the lids.

5 Sterilise at once, preferably in a pressure cooker. The temperature should reach 240° F. This temperature is indicated on the pressure gauge, i.e. 10-15 lb and should be kept there for 35-40 minutes to ensure complete sterilisation. The cooker is then allowed to cool down completely before the lid is removed. These pressure cookers (Easiwork or Pentecon) are of a special type and are fitted with a gauge. Unfortunately, few people possess one and so one has to fall back on the water bath method. Vegetables preserved by this method, a much longer one, have not the flavour of those sterilised by pressure cooker.

WATER- ATH METHOD

1 Blanch vegetables as directed. Have ready the hot, scrupulously clean jars and fill with the vegetables, leaving a half inch gap at the top.

2 Fill with boiling blanching water, adding half a teaspoon

of salt to each pound jar, and making up with fresh boiling water if necessary.

3 Seal down at once and put into steriliser, cover with hot water, making sure that the water comes at least 3-4 inches over the tops of the jars.

4 Bring to the boil and boil hard for 3 hours, counting the time from when the water boils.

Note: When you are bottling vegetables, choose small jars to ensure that the heat will penetrate to the centre of the jar.

LEMON JUICE OR ACID-BRINE METHOD

1 Here great care must be taken to see that the bottles or jars are scrupulously clean. Choose small jars and new rubber rings. Heat jars.

2 Pick over and wash vegetables carefully.

3 Prepare acid-brine solution with:

4 pints water: 1 level tablespoon salt: $\frac{3}{4}$ pint (12 liquid ounces) strained lemon juice: for peas, take 1 pint lemon juice, the same proportions of water and salt, and 1 tablespoon sugar.

4 Dissolve salt in the water and add lemon juice.

5 Put the vegetables into a pan, cover well with the solution, bring to the boil and boil 6-10 minutes. Then pack hot into the hot jars, not too tightly, and fill with the boiling solution to the brim. Seal at once.

6 Put the jars at once into a steriliser of boiling water, making sure that the tops are covered with at least 2 inches of water.

7 Boil hard for $1\frac{1}{2}$ hours for 1 lb jars and 2 hours for 2 lb jars.

8 Screw tops down securely. The liquid in the jars should cover the vegetables. If any are uncovered, open and

use straight away. Do not attempt to fill up and re-sterilise.

9 To use – turn out contents of bottle with the liquid into a pan; if there is not enough liquid to cover, add water. Boil hard for 15 minutes, stirring occasionally. Then drain, add butter and serve. A pinch of bi-carbonate of soda may be added to the boiling water to counteract the acid flavour.

10 If any bottles or jars have an unpleasant smell and have gone bad, do not taste, but bury or burn.

CANNING

BY HOM-CAN OR DIXIE CANNING MACHINES

Fruit and vegetables can be canned: fruit in a hot-water-steriliser and vegetables in a pressure cooker.

Preliminary preparation

As for bottling, fruit should be chosen with care, be ripe but firm, and should be prepared as for cooking, i.e. topped and tailed, in some cases peeled, stoned and sometimes halved, in every event carefully washed and examined for blemishes.

Vegetables should be young and fresh; they also should be prepared as for cooking.

Apparatus for home canning usually includes a booklet of instructions – *this should be carefully read and followed with exactitude*. The directions for sealing the cans, in particular, must be exactly followed for successful canning.

First of all, soak cans and lids in boiling water for 2-3 minutes to sterilise them. Drain well and set on a tray.

Fill the cans with fruit or vegetables to within $\frac{1}{4}$ inch of the top and pack fairly firmly, using the handle of a wooden spoon or spatula. Tap the bottom of the can on the table to settle the contents.

Fill to within ⅛ inch of the brim of the can with boiling water or syrup, and be sure it *is* boiling. Have a boiling kettle at hand, or a saucepan of boiling syrup, fill one can at a time and seal it *at once*. This is important.

Lift the can on to the stand of your canning machine with a folded cloth, or with tongs (these are very useful in bottling and canning), and seal as directed in the HOM-CAN booklet.

Take the can and plunge it at once into a large container of fast-boiling water. Boil rapidly for 23-25 minutes, consulting the chart overleaf. If, after all the cans are in, they take some minutes (say 10) to come to the boil, deduct this time from the time allowed for sterilising.

Lift out the cans with tongs and plunge them into cold water. A deep sink is convenient for this soaking, and the tap should be allowed to run for some minutes to cool the cans quickly. When they are quite cold, lift them out, dry them, write the contents on the tin with the pencil specially provided by the Home Canning Equipment Co. for this purpose, add the date, and store the tins in a cool, dry place.

Syrup for filling the cans of fruit varies according to the acidity of the fruit. The strength should be the same as that used in bottling.

Vegetables are filled into the tins in the same way, and the tins are then placed in a large pressure cooker, on a rack, and sterilised for the times specified on the chart. When the time has elapsed, they are lifted out of the cooker and plunged into running cold water. The water in the pressure cooker should cover the rack – for over 30 minutes pressure cooking, allow 1 pint of boiling water for safety's sake.

All vegetables are pre-cooked or blanched for a time before canning. See directions on chart.

TIME TABLE FOR STERILISING CANNED FRUIT
(LARGE 2½ SIZE)

(Deduct time taken to come again to the boil after cans have been put into steriliser).

Fruit	Boiling Time in Minutes
Apples (packed raw in liquid)	20
Apricots	25
Blackberries	22
Currants, red and white	22
Damsons, stone if desired	25
Gooseberries	22
Grapes	24
Loganberries	22
Mulberries	22
Nectarines	25
Peaches, stoned, in halves	25
Ripe Plums	22
Raspberries	22
Rhubarb	24
Strawberries	22
Unripe Plums	25
Black Currants	22
Cherries	25
Pears, peeled and cut in halves or slices	25
Pineapple, peeled, cut in slices	30
Quinces	30
Figs, fresh, with lemon juice	75
Tomatoes, whole in brine	40
Tomatoes, pulped	50

Preparation	Time in Cooker in Minutes 10 lb pressure
Asparagus Pre-cook 3 minutes, add water used in cooking.	30
French Beans Pre-cook 1 minute, add cooking water.	25
Peas Pre-cook 3-7 minutes according to size, add cooking water.	40
Mushrooms Blanch 5 minutes, add water and lemon juice.	25
Celery Trim, cut and pack; add boiling water.	30

You are strongly recommended to boil all home-canned vegetables for 10 minutes before serving them. This rule does not apply to tomatoes, which are regarded as fruit.

*

CHAPTER VI

Home Preserving

THIS TITLE covers a variety of recipes, all of which can be added to your store cupboard. As will be seen, the subjects vary from the drying of herbs to the making of fruit syrups.

Other recipes included are for more immediate consumption, and hail from the Continent as well as from England. These make for interest and variety in the daily menu.

The first recipe is for salting beans: these make a welcome vegetable in the winter months and are excellent if properly salted and treated afterwards. Store them in a cool place in larder or cellar.

SALTING BEANS

The beans used may be either French or runner beans. Leave whole or slice, according to size. The salt must be good quality block salt and ground down before use. Weigh beans and salt in order to get the right proportion of each. Failure to do this may mean that the beans will not keep. Use large earthernware or glass jars, or small crocks with lids.

To use the beans, wash 5 or 6 times in cold water. Then pour on scalding hot water and leave to soak for about an hour and a half, not longer. Rinse again, put into boiling unsalted water and cook until tender, for about half an hour. Drain and finish off with a good lump of butter.

If you wish you may add a good pinch of bi-carbonate of soda to the cooking water.

To Salt Beans

To 3 lb prepared beans take 1 lb ground block salt. Wash beans thoroughly, dry, top and tail, and string if necessary. If tender, French beans snap in two or three pieces; if they are small, leave whole. Slice runner beans.

Have ready the jars or crock, put a layer of salt in the bottom, about ½ inch. Cover with the prepared beans, scatter over a layer of salt and continue until all the beans are used. Finish with a layer of salt. Cover jar with a plate and leave for 48 hours, pressing down occasionally as the beans shrink and become wet. Then fill up with more beans and salt in proportion, always leaving with a layer of salt on top.

When the jars are full (and this is important), tie down securely with three layers of greaseproof paper.

The beans should keep sweet and good for several months.

Sauerkraut

Sauerkraut is cabbage preserved partly by salting and partly by fermentation. The hard white cabbage is the most satisfactory.

Trim the cabbage, cut into four, remove most of the hard stalk, then cut down into very fine shreds. Pack into a large stone crock or wooden tub in layers with salt, in proportion, not more than about 2-3 oz per 5 lb cabbage. Cover the top with cabbage leaves, press down well. Cover with a piece of muslin and put a wooden board on the top with a heavy weight on it. Leave in a warm place between 70° and 78° for 2 to 3 weeks to allow fermentation to take place. Drain off the liquid. If the sauerkraut is not for immediate use, pack into bottling jars when all fermentation has ceased, and sterilise for 40 minutes with the lid on the pan and the bottles well screwed or clipped down. Keep in a cool place till required.

Tomato purée is a most welcome addition to the store-cupboard. It is extremely useful for flavouring soups, stews, sauces and cream salad dressing. The essential of a good purée is that it should be thick and concentrated, the consistency should be that of a fruit butter. It should be made when tomatoes are plentiful and cheap and fully ripe. The following recipes give two ways of preserving the purée, one by sterilising and the other by coating with oil. This latter recipe is extremely good, but calls for a fair quantity of tomatoes. It is highly concentrated as the purée must be almost solid when cold, otherwise the oil will seep through and so spoil the contents of the jar.

Tomato Purée (1)

To every 4 lb tomatoes add 1 chopped onion, 1 clove of garlic, 3 large sprigs of parsley, a sprig of thyme and a bayleaf, salt, and freshly ground pepper to taste.

Wash tomatoes, cut in half and put into a preserving pan with the onion, garlic and herbs tied together. Heat on a slow fire, bruising well with a wooden spoon. When a pulp forms add seasoning to taste, but do not season too highly as the reduction will concentrate the flavour. Continue to simmer for a further 45 minutes or until the whole mixture is very soft, then rub through a nylon sieve, first removing the herbs.

Put the pulp back into the cleaned pan and boil, stirring frequently until well reduced. Pour this into hot small jars with screw-top lids (honey jars are suitable for this), then sterilise them for 45 minutes.

The jars must be stood on the stand in the bottom of the steriliser or on a piece of wood or wire at the bottom of a pan. Fill with water ⅜ of the way up the jar, cover the pan, bring slowly to the boil and boil gently for the time prescribed.

Tomato Purée (2)

24 lb ripe tomatoes: 1 bunch basil or lemon thyme: 1 level teaspoon salt and 1 level teaspoon sugar per pint of purée.

Wipe the tomatoes, cut in half and squeeze into a strainer to remove the seeds and water. Rub this pulp in the strainer with a spoon to extract all liquid. Put this into a preserving pan with the tomatoes and herbs. Simmer to a pulp, remove herbs, and rub through a hair or nylon sieve. Measure purée and add salt and sugar in the proportion given. Return to the cleaned pan, and boil gently and steadily until very thick.

For the last 15-20 minutes of boiling, the purée must be continually stirred otherwise it will burn. Turn into small pots and wipe the edges round well. When cold, run an ⅛ inch of olive oil over the top and cover with paper.

This is an easy and safe way of preserving the purée but it must be really thick, in fact quite solid when cold. When wanted for use, pour off oil, take what is required, smooth over the surface, and pour over fresh oil.

Pickled Eggs

These are not well known, but are delicious to eat with

cheese for a packed lunch, in sandwiches or as a 'side' dish to serve with cold meats.

They will be ready to eat after 3 to 4 weeks in pickle.

12 hard-boiled eggs: spiced vinegar: 2 hot chillies.

For the spiced vinegar: 1½-2 pints white vinegar: ½ oz root ginger, bruised: ½ oz white peppercorns: ½ oz allspice.

Simmer vinegar with the spices tied in muslin until well flavoured. Allow to cool. Remove shells carefully from eggs. Arrange in jars, put a piece of chilli in each jar. Cover completely with the spiced vinegar. Tie down securely.

Best pickled in Kilner jars.

Horse-Radish

Horse-radish is a most useful root to preserve for the winter and if home-made has much more flavour than the bought variety and is of course much cheaper. Most gardens have a root or two of horse-radish to spare for winter use or some may be bought for this purpose.

Use white vinegar as this will keep the horse-radish a better colour.

Wash, peel and grate the roots at once. Fill into small jars about two-thirds full. Add a level teaspoon salt and ½ teaspoon sugar to each jar with a small piece of fresh chilli. Fill to the top with white vinegar. If you wish you may use a spiced vinegar. Cover well with paper or screw down the lid, but make sure the lid is lined with paper so that the metal does not come in contact with the vinegar.

For use – strain off the vinegar and press the horse-radish lightly to remove any surplus liquid. It is then ready for use in a sauce or may be sprinkled over a beet-root salad, etc.

Keep the vinegar for salad dressings or for adding to spiced vinegar for pickles.

Flavoured Vinegars

These are excellent to have both for salad dressings, to use for sousing fish and for pickles.

They are so much cheaper to make than to buy and a greater variety can be made at home than can be bought in the shops.

They are very simple to make. The most useful are tarragon, mixed herbs, mint, chilli and garlic. Use white wine or white distilled vinegar.

Tarragon Vinegar

French tarragon must be used. This herb has a delicate but pungent scent of aniseed and makes perhaps the most popular of all the flavoured vinegars. Like all these vinegars a little should be added to ordinary vinegar when making a dressing.

To 1 pint of tarragon leaves picked from their stalks, take 1½ pints vinegar. Put the leaves, lightly bruised, into a jar, pour the cold vinegar over, cover closely and leave for 2-3 weeks. Then strain through muslin, pour off into bottles and cork tightly. If the vinegar does not taste strongly of tarragon, leave for a few days longer before straining off.

The herbs should be picked just before flowering, early to mid-summer. The same applies to the following two recipes.

94

Herb Vinegar

Take chives, marjoram, tarragon and parsley in equal quantities. Remove stalks and chop not too finely. Use 4 heaped tablespoons to a pint of vinegar. Put together into a jar, cover closely and leave 2-3 weeks. Strain through a piece of muslin and then bottle.

Mint Vinegar

This is useful as a basis for mint sauce. Pack a quart measure full of mint leaves. Turn into a larger jar or crock. Pour on 2 pints vinegar, cover closely and leave for three weeks. Strain off and bottle.

Chilli Vinegar

Preferably red chillies should be used for this, as they are riper and therefore hotter. Green, however, will do, though the time for infusion may be a little longer.

Split the chillies in half, taking about 50 to a quart of vinegar. Boil the vinegar, put in the chillies and reboil. Turn all into a jar or crock, cover and leave for 5 to 6 weeks. Strain off and bottle.

Garlic Vinegar

8 to 9 cloves of garlic – this represents approximately one root: 1 pint wine vinegar.

Peel cloves. Crush under a knife or in a mortar. Bring vinegar to the boil and pour on to the garlic. Leave to stand for two weeks, then strain off and bottle.

Summer Vinegar

Nasturtium flowers: white wine vinegar: salt: $\frac{1}{2}$ teaspoon cayenne pepper.

Pick the flowers on a dry day and fill a large Kilner jar pressing them down well; add a good pinch of salt and the cayenne, cover with the cold vinegar and cover tightly. After a day or two, fill the jar with extra vinegar and leave for at least 10 days.

Good with fish.

Cress Vinegar

½ oz cress seed: 1 quart white wine vinegar or white distilled vinegar.

Dry and pound the seeds (the kind sown in the garden with mustard) and then pour over the vinegar. Leave standing for 10 days, stirring well or shaking it up every day. Strain through muslin, pour off into bottles and cork tightly.

This vinegar is excellent for dressings for salads and cold meat.

Blackberry Vinegar

4 lb blackberries: 2 quarts white distilled vinegar: loaf sugar.

Place the blackberries in an earthenware crock or bowl and cover with the vinegar. Let it stand in a warm place for three days. Stir night and morning with a wooden spoon.

Strain through a jelly bag or double muslin, and to every pint of juice add 1 lb sugar. Stir over a low heat until the sugar is dissolved, then boil rapidly for 15 minutes, skimming well. Allow to cool and then bottle.

Raspberry Vinegar

4 lb raspberries: 1 quart vinegar (white distilled): pre-

serving or loaf sugar.

Bruise raspberries lightly, put them into an earthenware crock or bowl with the vinegar. Allow to stand for a week. Stir every day with a wooden spoon.

Strain through a jelly bag or fine cloth. Measure juice and add 1 lb sugar to 1 pint of juice. Stir over slow fire until sugar is dissolved, then boil rapidly for 15 minutes, skimming well. Then cool and bottle.

Two to three tablespoons in a tumbler with soda or plain water added makes a very refreshing drink.

Cucumber Vinegar

This vinegar is good for sousing salmon, white fish or for dressing fish salads.

1 dozen cucumbers, ridge or outdoor: 3 medium-sized onions: ½ teaspoon cayenne pepper: 1 tablespoon salt: 2½ pints vinegar.

Peel and slice cucumbers and onions. Put them into the vinegar and bring to the boil. Add the cayenne and salt. Boil for 2 minutes, turn into a jar or bowl, cover closely and leave for 10 days. Drain off and bottle.

Sweet vinegars, such as the liquid in which spiced fruits have been preserved, are excellent for adding as flavouring to dressings, mayonnaise, etc.

DRYING HERBS

Herbs for drying should be picked just before flowering. The best and most useful sorts are parsley, mint, thyme (both lemon and ordinary), marjoram, sage, savory. The two former may be kept separately when dried and powdered, the former for general use and the latter for pea or lentil soups in winter. The other herbs are usually mixed, when dried, in proportion to the strength of flavour. After they have been dried and powdered, herbs should be kept in small airtight tins or jars appropriately labelled.

Gather herbs on a dry day but not in full sun. Pick over and, in the case of thyme and savory, wash and dry. Tie these herbs in bundles and hang up in an airing cupboard overnight or until dry and brittle. If an airing cupboard is not available, hang up above the stove rack or lay on the rack covered by muslin or a piece of paper.

When the leaves are thoroughly dry strip them off the stalks, crush lightly with the fingers or with a rolling pin, and store as directed above.

Parsley

Wash and dry thoroughly. Pick leaves from the stalks and lay on sheets of paper or on a muslin tray (see fruit drying). Put in a warm place as before or in a very cool oven (the cool oven of the Aga for example), but the heat must not rise more than 125° F. Turn the parsley over from time to time. If the heat is constant and kept at about 100° F., the parsley will dry in a short space of time, in a day or less. The quicker it dries, the better the colour. Another method is to dry the parsley in a hot oven at 370°-380° F. for one minute. This is a little more tricky as care must be taken that the parsley does not scorch, and the colour and flavour spoil.

Mint

Better colour will be obtained if the leaves are tied in a piece of muslin and dipped into boiling water for one minute. Drain well, spread out on muslin and dry in a temperature not greater than 125°-130° F.

The leaves should be dry in about 1½ hours. Immediately they are crisp and brittle, crush and store. If you wish you may sift the leaves through a coarse wire sieve to remove any small stalks or fibres.

Treat sage, basil, etc. in the same way.

FRUIT SYRUPS

These are not made often nowadays, which is a pity, as they are an asset to have in the store-cupboard. Pleasant to the taste, they make excellent sauces to serve with puddings, for flavouring sweets or as a basis for fruit drinks.

Blackcurrant syrup is soothing for a cold in winter, and other flavours make delicious iced fruit cups for parties.

If syrups are to be made regularly it is well worth while investing in special bottles in which to store them. The best are the lever stoppered type with a china cap and rubber washer. The latter has to be renewed every year, but they are easy to handle, the general appearance of the bottle is good and, with care, they can be used year after year. They are obtainable in pint sizes. Another suitable bottle is the sauce bottle with a screw cap; this is obtainable in smaller sizes.

The rules for making a syrup are similar to those of jelly-making. The juice from the fruit is extracted in gentle heat; here a little water is usually employed. The resulting juice is measured when cold, and the sugar added and stirred until dissolved. It should then be bottled immediately and sterilised.

Store in a cool dark place. Light will cause the colour of the syrup to fade. A little colouring may be added to deepen the colour of pale syrup and certainly improves the appearance and attractiveness of the syrup.

Syrup made from Soft Berried Fruits

Raspberries, currants, strawberries, elderberries, blackberries and loganberries can be used singly or as a mixture, such as raspberries and redcurrants. Choose fresh clean ripe fruit and avoid washing if possible. Pick well over and discard any mouldy or blemished fruits. Turn into a double saucepan and add ¼ to ½ pint of water according to the firmness of the fruit. For example, ¼ pint for raspberries or strawberries and ½ pint for blackcurrants. Cook for about an hour, crushing the fruit down at intervals. When the mixture is thoroughly soft turn it into a cheese cloth or jelly bag to drain. Leave overnight until all the juice has run through. Then measure and add ¾ lb cane preserving or loaf sugar to each pint of juice. Stir occasionally until dissolved. Strain again through a piece of muslin, pour at once into bottles and seal down.

Stand the bottles in a steriliser and fill with cold water to cover. Heat slowly so that a temperature of 170°-175° is reached in one hour, i.e. about simmering point. Keep at this temperature for 20-30 minutes according to the size of the bottles. Remove, cool, label and store.

If a double saucepan is not available, use an ordinary saucepan, preferably enamel, and draw out the juice as slowly as possible.

Fruit with little colour or flavour, such as gooseberries and apples, make an excellent basic syrup for other flavours. The following recipe is an example of this.

Muscat Syrup

This is so called as the flavour is that of muscat grapes. It is delicious for fresh fruit compôtes, water ices, drinks and so on. Use an ordinary saucepan or preserving pan for this.

3 lb green gooseberries: ½ pint water: 2 lb, 12 oz loaf sugar: about 8 large elderflowers, washed but left on the stalks.

Top and tail and wash gooseberries, put them into a pan with the water and simmer gently until soft, but without breaking the fruit. Add the warmed sugar, allow to dissolve and bring up to the boil. Tie the elderflowers in a piece of muslin and add to the syrup. Draw aside and allow to infuse for 7-10 minutes. Then strain all through muslin.

Bottle syrup and sterilise.

The gooseberries may be used for a purée or a fool, etc.

Rose Hip Syrup

This, as a rich source of Vitamin C, is much cheaper to make than to buy. Use as for the bought product, i.e., 2 teaspoonsful of syrup daily. It is best stored in small bottles.

2½ lb ripe red rose hips, wash and remove the calyces. Put through a mincer and pour on 3 pints boiling water. Turn into a pan and bring up to the boil. Draw aside and stand for 15 minutes. Strain through a jelly bag or muslin. Measure juice and, if more than 1½ pints, boil down in a clean pan until the juice measures that amount. Add 1¼ lb sugar, allow to dissolve, then boil hard for 5 minutes. Bottle when cold and sterilise as for the other syrups.

Candied Orange Peel

Use skins with the juicy pulp removed, and preferably the thick-skinned variety of orange. To the skins of three large oranges allow:

6 oz granulated sugar: $\frac{3}{4}$ gill water: 1 large tablespoonful golden syrup.

Cover the skins with cold water. Bring to the boil, drain. Repeat this process twice more. With a sharp-edged spoon, gently scrape out the remains of the orange pulp, leaving the white pith intact. Then cover afresh with cold water, adding a pinch of bicarbonate of soda. Boil uncovered until the skins are tender. Drain.

Candied peel is well worth making during the autumn months ready for Christmas cakes and puddings. It is also a great economy.

Put the sugar, water and syrup into a pan. Dissolve and bring to the boil. Add the peels, simmer with the lid off the pan until most of the syrup is absorbed and the peels are clear. Turn into a jar and tie down with paper or stopper closely. This peel will keep a comparatively short time, approximately six weeks. For longer keeping, the peel should be candied properly, i.e put on wire trays and basted with syrup, boiled down to a certain degree, and then subjected to gentle heat.

The above recipe is perfectly suited to ordinary domestic use. If, just before use, the peel is found to be too wet and sticky, the pieces may be put on to a wire rack and dried off in a cool oven.

Note: Treat lemon peel in the same way but double the quantity of sugar etc. for three grapefruit.

DRYING FRUIT

When there is a glut of apples, plums or pears, it is of great advantage to dry them, as they take little room to store and are cheap to prepare. The equipment necessary is simple, the most essential being wooden frames over which butter muslin can be stretched, and an even source of heat such as an oven, airing cupboard, etc. An oven thermometer also ensures success.

The trays are made simply by nailing four pieces of wood together to form a square, and stretching pieces of butter muslin or cheese cloth over and tacking them down.

For apple rings, bamboo canes are needed. Sliced apples can be dried on the muslin.

Fruit

Apples, pears, plums are the most suitable for drying. The fruit should be perfectly sound and quite ripe.

To prepare: For apples – peel, core and cut into rings about ¼ inch thick or quarter and cut into thick slices. Drop at once into slightly salted water, 1 tablespoon to 1 quart water, to prevent discolouration.

Treat pears in the same way but leave in quarters.

For plums – either leave whole or cut in half and remove stones. Remember that fruit shrinks very much in drying, so choose the large, firm, fleshy type of plum. If left whole and dried a little more slowly, they will resemble prunes and are delicious. After blanching, dry thoroughly in clean cloths, thread apple rings on to the canes and arrange the sliced apple and pears on the muslin trays close together, but without touching one another.

Arrange plums in the same way. Place trays or canes in the oven, having first got it to the required temperature.

To dry: The most important part of this process is that the heat should be very gradual, otherwise a skin will form on the outside and so harden the fruit. In the case of plums, too much heat would cause the skins to burst. The temperature for drying varies from about 120° F. to about 145° F. Always start at the lowest temperature and keep at that for the first hour, then increase to 140°F. Keep at that temperature until the fruits are dried; this will take from between 3 to 6 hours, according to the size of the fruit. Oven temperatures are more easily controlled than that of an airing cupboard, etc. The fruit when properly dried should be soft, pliable and springy in texture. No moisture should be present when the fruit is pressed, though it must not be dry and brittle in any way.

To condition: After drying, the fruit must be conditioned by being spread out on clean paper to cool. Cover with muslin or paper and leave in a dark cool place for 12 hours. Turn them over two or three times during this period.

To store: Pack carefully into glass jars, clean metal boxes, etc. Ensure that they are completely airtight by using a screw type lid on the jar, or sealing round the tin lid with adhesive tape.

Store in a very dry room or cupboard.

Potted Mushrooms

1½ lb very fresh button mushrooms: 3 oz butter: salt, pepper, ground mace and cayenne: 1 large tablespoon anchovy essence: clarified butter or mutton fat.

Wipe mushrooms carefully to remove any grit. Put into a scrupulously clean saucepan and cook slowly until the juice runs, then increase heat until all juice has disappeared. Then add the butter, seasoning and spice. Cook until the butter is absorbed, then add the anchovy essence. Cook gently for a little longer, then press into small bowls or pots. Cool and run over clarified butter or fat.

Note: These mushrooms are not for storing for any length of time, but should be eaten within a month or so. Store in a cool place.

★

CHAPTER VII

Drinks and Syrups

Claret Cup (1)

VERY REFRESHING FOR HOT DAYS

1 bottle claret: 2 bottles soda water: 1 large tablespoon castor sugar: sliced lemon.

Stir all together and ice well.

The soda water bottles should be the large size, i.e. a pint or more.

Claret Cup (2)

1 bottle claret: 2 bottles soda water: 2-3 lumps of sugar: a lemon: a large glass of sherry: a sprig of borage or mint.

Chill the wine and soda water thoroughly in the bottles before mixing.

About a quarter of an hour before serving, rub off the zest of the lemon on to the lump sugar. Pour wine and soda into a jug, add the sugar, stir to dissolve. Then add the sherry, the juice of half the lemon, and sugar to taste, if you wish.

Put in the borage or mint and keep well chilled until the cup is served. Then take out the borage.

Note: Claret cups have gone somewhat out of fashion nowadays. They were most popular in the latter part of the nineteenth century. Nowadays, claret is so reasonable in price, that it is an excellent drink to serve at a buffet or for a dance.

Traditionally, this cup was always served in a silver or claret jug.

Strawberry Syrup

(For making jellies and fruit drinks.)

10 lb strawberries: 5 pints water: 4 oz tartaric acid: castor sugar.

Hull the berries and put into a large bowl. Add the acid to the water and pour over the fruit. Leave for 24 hours. Strain through a jelly bag or a piece of linen. The next day, measure the juice and put 1½ lb of sugar to each pint of juice. Stir until dissolved, strain through a muslin and bottle, corking it well down or using a special syrup bottle with a clip seal. Store in a cool dark place.

Use raspberries to make a raspberry syrup.

Ginger Beer

2 gallons water: 3½ lb loaf sugar: the rind and juice of 4 lemons: 2 oz root ginger, well pounded: 1 egg white: 2 tablespoons yeast.

Boil all together, with the exception of the lemon juice and yeast, for 10 minutes. Pour into a large crock to cool. Add the lemon juice, and when the liquid is 'milk warm' put in the yeast. Leave for 24 hours. Strain into a small cask and after 3-4 days close it. Bottle the liquid in 3 weeks and it will be ready to drink 3 weeks after that.

When making ginger beer in this way, it is advisable to buy a new wooden cask. Fill it with cold water for 2 or 3 days, then empty, and allow to dry for a day or two before use.

Barley Water

2 oz pearl barley: rind and juice of 2 lemons: 2 quarts water: 10 lumps sugar.

Wash barley and put into a pan with the water. Put the thinly pared rind of the lemons and the juice into a jug with the sugar.

Bring the water and barley slowly to the boil, and simmer for 5 minutes. Then pour the contents of the pan into the jug. When cold, strain off and use.

Lemonade Syrup – for Diluting

6 lemons: 3 lb loaf sugar: 1 oz citric acid: ½ oz tartaric acid: 3 quarts water.

Put the sugar, citric and tartaric acid in a basin and pour over the boiling water and stir well until the sugar is melted. Add the juice of the lemons and the rinds of three of them cut into very fine strips.

Stand overnight, then strain and bottle.

Summer Drink

1 oz pearl barley: 1 quart boiling water: the juice of 1 lemon and the pared rind of half: sugar to taste: 2 wine-glasses sherry.

Wash barley, put into a jug with the lemon rind and juice. Pour on the water and leave until cold. Then strain off, sweeten to taste and add the sherry.

Ice with a sprig of mint in the jug.

INDEX